CHAPTER I

Caring About Ourselves

THE CHALLENGE

Cathleen Crowell's parents fought, separated and eventually divorced when she was a little girl. Like many youngsters in that situation she blamed herself for this marital discord, once telling her teddy bear, "It's all my fault my daddy and mommy don't like each other anymore."

The resulting poor self-image caused her to develop an excessive fear of being left out, rejected or punished. To avoid these dreaded disasters, Cathy began at an early age to concoct lies, even complicated ones, in an effort to escape punishment or to gain permission for some activity which otherwise might be prohibited.

In her teen years she also turned to promiscuous sexual activity as a way of compensating for her low self-esteem. Later, Cathleen would reflect and comment, "Those sexual experiences gave me something to be good at, or at least that's what I told myself. And I felt sort of loved. Stupid, isn't it?"

After one episode, she feared a possible pregnancy and made up a story about rape, thereby hoping to cover the situation if her worries materialized. However, the alibi got out of hand, leading her to accuse someone falsely of the supposed offense. Her apparently perjured testimony sent the man to prison, until years later when she publicly revoked her original accusation.

The tragedies of this troubled woman's life indicate among other things that failure to care deeply about ourselves can lead to very destructive behavior. A poor self-image or lack of proper self-esteem often unwittingly pushes us to hurt ourselves and others.[1]

THE RESPONSE

To Cathy Crowell and those who struggle with similar negative images of themselves, the Roman Catholic Church might well cite these biblical words which God spoke to the Old Testament prophet Isaiah: *"You are precious in my eyes and glorious and . . . I love you."*[2] That statement in effect says, "You are unique, special and therefore good." Why? Because you have been made by God and saved by Christ.

1

MADE BY GOD

Each Sunday at Mass after the sermon or homily, Catholics stand and recite the Profession of Faith, a formula of beliefs or creed handed down from the early Church. The opening words are: *"We believe in one God, the Father, the Almighty, maker of heaven and earth, of all that is seen and unseen."*

That faith in a great and loving God who created all things from nothing is frequently expressed in the official words of worship. For example, later on after the creed, the presiding priest may use this phrase, *"Father, you are holy indeed, and all creation rightly gives you praise . . . all life, all holiness comes from you . . ."* Or he might employ this text, *"You alone are God, living and true . . . Source of life and goodness, you have created all things."*[3]

The Catholic Church believes that every human being has been made by God. While, obviously, parents are the cooperating instruments, the Church holds that our invisible spiritual part or soul requires a direct act of creation by the Maker. We reflect within us, therefore, divine qualities, such as immortality; for in the words of the first biblical book, Genesis, we have been made in God's *image* and *likeness.*

Moreover, everything God made and makes is good. Again, to quote Genesis in the story describing the creation of the world, God looked over all creation, including Adam and Eve, the first parents, and saw that it was *very good.*

In the words of a popular bumper-sticker slogan, *"God does not make junk."*[4]

Jesus reiterated this truth about our uniqueness before God when, in urging us not to worry but rather to trust in God's providence, he observed, *"Consider the ravens: They do not reap, they have neither cellar nor barn yet God feeds them. How much more important you are than the birds!"*[5]

PRACTICAL CONSEQUENCES

This belief in the specialness and goodness of all creation, including and especially human beings, has led to a consistent **ethic of life** approach to contemporary moral issues. The Catholic Church holds that all human life is sacred, from inside the womb until final rest within a tomb. Thus it opposes both abortion at one end of the spectrum and euthanasia, which directly terminates an elderly or critically ill individual, at the opposite end of the continuum. On in-between questions Catholic bishops have spoken publicly against the potential violence of the arms race and also expressed a preferential option for the poor who wage a daily battle simply to survive.

SAVED BY CHRIST

Two facts about the human condition can cloud this picture of our essential goodness as God's uniquely created persons: the past personal mistakes we have made and the present unruly impulses within us.

Once we reach the age of reason, it becomes clear that we are free to make choices. The Catholic Church has always taught that humans possess this fundamental freedom, even though our responsibility for certain actions may be lessened because of various factors. However, that liberty enables us to make negative choices as well as positive ones, select evil instead of good, slip into vices rather than acquire virtues. We, in fact, can and do sin.

Moreover, we sense all too well that a certain war goes on within us. In his letter to the Romans, St. Paul summarized this tension when he remarked, *"I cannot even under-*

stand my own actions. I do not do what I want to do but what I hate . . . what happens is that I do, not the good I will to do, but the evil I do not intend . . . my inner self agrees with the law of God, but I see in my body's members another law at war with the law of my mind; this makes me the prisoner of sin in my members."[6]

Those desires or impulses which strongly push or pull us in contrary directions would appear to indicate that our human nature is flawed or wounded. The Church labels this phenomenon an effect of *original sin*, an inherited weakness not of our own doing but which nevertheless requires help and healing. Genesis' story about the fall of Adam and Eve in the Garden dramatizes this readily recognized experience of the weakened human condition and our need for assistance in overcoming the effects of original sin.

DEATH TO LIFE

That double burden—personal sins and unruly tendencies—far from damaging our self-esteem can, in the Church's mind, lead us to an even deeper understanding of how precious we are in God's sight.

The Catholic Church teaches that Jesus, by his coming into this world and his living, suffering, dying and rising, has conquered the forces of darkness and death and introduced a kingdom of light and life. This suffering, death and resurrection of Christ are frequently termed the Paschal or Easter mystery. It means that the Savior has made it possible for all women and men to be forgiven their sins, to be healed of their weaknesses and eventually to reach a heavenly home of perma-nent, perfect happiness in the next world. God, indeed, wishes every person to be saved and to come to a knowledge of that truth.

This forgiveness, healing and salva-tion is a free, unearned gift. In the words of another bumper sticker: *"Christians are not saints, just saved."* The only requirements are that we be willing to accept this gift, that we believe in Jesus Christ as Savior, as the promised one who came to deliver us, and that we be willing to be baptized in his name. The Savior's own words are crucial here:

"No one can enter into God's kingdom without being begotten of water and Spirit."[7]

Baptism

The Church views Baptism as a death and resurrection experience. We die to sin and rise to life. We put aside our old self and put on a new person. We bury our past shadows and bad tendencies and emerge into a life of light and goodness. St. Paul mentions this notion in his letter to the Romans:

"Are you not aware that we who were baptized into Christ Jesus were baptized into his death? Through baptism into his death we were buried with him, so that, just as Christ was raised from the dead by the glory of the Father, we too might live a new life. If we have been united with him through likeness to his death, so shall we be through a like resurrection."[8]

However, the Church also sees Baptism as an initiation, a welcoming of the person into the Christian family, a rite which joins the baptized to a community of believers linked together by ties of faith, grace and love.

The ceremonies of Baptism naturally reflect both that concept of becoming a member of the Church and the death/resurrection effect of this ritual.

Water

The Church prefers that those being baptized, infants or adults, ideally should be immersed in water while the words are pronounced, *"I baptize you in the name of the Father, and of the Son, and of the Holy Spirit."* Several of the older basilicas in Rome, Italy, provide for this possibility and many newer churches in the United States have constructed baptismal fonts which make it feasible. In those situations, the person is at least partially submerged in the water and then rises from it as a Christian. That expresses the burial and resurrection concept well. However, the Church also allows the water simply to be poured over the forehead.

EASTER AND SUNDAYS

Easter is **the** Christian feast or celebration recalling and rejoicing over Jesus' victory over death and sin. Each Sunday, furthermore, is viewed as a little Easter. Since Baptism connects us to Christ's victorious action, the Church urges that normally the baptismal ceremonies be held on Sundays.

WHITE GARMENT

After the actual Baptism, the new Christian is clothed with a white garment symbolic of the transformation which has taken place. That symbolism is carried over years later into the funeral services of the baptized person when a white cloth or pall is spread over the casket in church as a reminder of Baptism which opens the way to a new life forever after death.

CANDLE

A large Easter or Paschal candle is lighted on Holy Saturday night as a symbol of Jesus, the light of the world, conquering forever the powers of darkness. It remains in the church through the fifty days after Easter during which we celebrate the Resurrection. It is also used at Baptisms. Following the imposition of the garment, a smaller taper is lighted from the larger Paschal candle and given to the newly baptized or the parents. The Church encourages this baptismal candle to be lighted every year at home on the anniversary of the person's Baptism as a reminder of the important event.

PROMISES

The one to be baptized or the parents and godparents explicitly promise during the ceremony to reject sin, evil and Satan, the prince of darkness, and to believe in God, Jesus, the Church and life everlasting. Those promises are repeated every year on Easter Sunday to remind us of the significance of our Baptism and to recall to our minds that as part of a Christian Family we are making this journey with many sisters and brothers who care about us and share our ideals.

SIGN OF THE CROSS AND HOLY WATER

Catholic Church entrances contain some type of vessels with holy or blessed water in them. The custom for Catholics is to dip the right hand into this font and then make the sign of the cross with the moistened finger(s). This is meant to be both a reminder of Baptism and an expression of faith in the Trinity of divine persons, for while making that gesture one silently says: *"In the name of the Father and of the Son and of the Holy Spirit."* It also naturally affirms our belief in Jesus' coming, dying and rising.

CREATED IN LOVE

Parents generally feel closest to their children when they are hurting or in some trouble. We could make the same comparison with God. The Lord loves us not in spite of our failures and weaknesses, but almost because of them, and God is never nearer than when we are burdened and broken hearted.

When at times we struggle like Cathleen Crowell with poor self-esteem and may tend not to care deeply about ourselves, two powerful truths of the Catholic Church can help us; we have been uniquely made by God and lovingly saved by Jesus Christ.

CHAPTER 2

The Search for Happiness

THE CHALLENGE

Franz Jaegerstaetter came into this world as an illegitimate child in 1907. He grew up in Upper Austria, working hard on a farm throughout the day and playing hard throughout the night.

With a gang of toughs he drank too much beer, fought often bloody battles against rival groups from other villages and sought to charm the area's female beauties. Quick thinking, enthusiastic and courageous, Franz emerged as the natural leader of these young ruffians.

For unknown reasons Franz left the village abruptly when he was 27 to work in some distant iron mines and during his three years there experienced a profound religious conversion.

Upon return to his native village, Jaegerstaetter married a devout young woman and to the amazement of the villagers, the former wild youth became a model husband and father. He resumed family farming, but his inner conversion continued.

Up at 5:30 each morning, Franz meditated and went to Mass before starting the day's strenuous labor in the fields. Regretful of his past wildness, the Austrian sought to do penance in reparation by giving up beer, fasting until noon each day and giving generously to the poor.

This new style of life brought peace and joy to the man. He would occasionally break into song while working in the fields, read the Bible while resting for a few moments under a tree and praise God while admiring the wonders of the Austrian countryside.

About that time the Nazi movement entered Austria. Jaegerstaetter judged Nazism to be a great evil and refused to cooperate with it in any way despite pleadings from his neighbors and friends to go along with the inevitable. Eventually he was imprisoned, sent to jail in Berlin and condemned to death by beheading.

Signing a supposedly uncompromising retraction would have brought release, but Franz refused. He told a Catholic chaplain visiting him at midnight before the execution day, "I am completely bound in inner union with the Lord, Father, and any reading would only interrupt that communication."

On the way to and at the scaffold, the chaplain noticed that Jaegerstaetter's eyes were shining with joy and confidence, and his face was radiant with peace and calm.

Later, the priest remarked, "The military beheaded a great man. I feel with certainty that this simple man is the only saint I have ever met in my lifetime."[1]

THE RESPONSE

Some 1500 years before this Austrian lived, another young man followed a somewhat similar pattern in his search for happiness. Augustine of Hippo likewise pursued a path of pleasure, and in doing so fathered a child out of wedlock. His mother, Monica, prayed with tears for twenty years to bring about his religious conversion. Finally, the North African realized that pure pleasure could not satisfy his quest and discovered the answer, as did Franz Jaegerstaetter, in a new relationship with God.

Later on, St. Augustine would write these famous words, *"Oh God, you have made us for yourself and our hearts are restless until they rest in you."*

Catholic youngsters several decades ago learned about their religion from small booklets called catechisms. There in question and answer form, they studied the major truths and practices of the Catholic Church.

An early question was: *"Why did God make you?"* The answer: *"God made me to know, love and serve him in this world and thus to be happy with him in the next."* Both Franz Jaegerstaetter and St. Augustine would probably agree that this response, while perhaps too simple and succinct for some, does, nevertheless, say it well.

THE NATURE OF GOD

Still, even if only God can satisfy the human heart and end our search for happiness, there are other questions: Who is God? What is God like? How does God fulfill our every desire?

The response to all these inquiries is necessarily elusive because God is a mystery, a being beyond us, an infinite reality never fully to be understood or comprehended. However, looking around at the world of nature, studying the Bible and listening to the words handed down to us by earlier believers gives us some partial answers to such questions.

We believe that God exists. God is one, and surpasses all positive

qualities imaginable. Thus we call God all powerful, knowing, wise, just, loving, good, forgiving and holy—to cite a few such characteristics. That makes our God distant and in a sense, far from us, exceeding human comprehension.

But we also believe that God reaches down and enters into our world and within our lives. God did so with the chosen Jewish people of the Old Testament or Hebrew Scriptures; God did so in sending Jesus Christ to and for us; God continues to do so today. Consequently, our God is at the same time distant and close.

We also believe that God is a personal being, mysteriously uniting both one and three, one divine nature and three divine persons—Father, Son and Holy Spirit. The Sign of the Cross, the prayer described in the last chapter, manifests that faith. The words *"In the name of"* (singular, one God) *"the Father, and of the Son and of the Holy Spirit"* (plural, three Persons) are accompanied by a gesture. It is traced from forehead to chest, then from left to right shoulders—forming a cross. The cross explicitly symbolizes our faith that he also rose from the dead, and sent the Spirit to lead us to the Father. This three-in-one characteristic of God we call the Trinity.

How does this mysterious God satisfy our hearts and fulfill our every desire? By providing partial happiness here on earth and promising perfect happiness in the life to come.

HAPPINESS HERE

In the last chapter we noted how God looked at all creation and judged that it was very good. The Catholic Church teaches, as a consequence, that by properly using these good things of this world our lives here on earth can be relatively happy and joyful. On the other hand, by improperly using those same good things we cause unhappiness and sorrow for ourselves and for others.

To foster a proper use of the created world and to eliminate or at least diminish an improper use of those things, the Church constantly incorporates the ordinary objects of nature into **prayer** and **worship.**

The Catholic Church has Jewish roots, and its official public prayer or liturgy reflects that heritage. Jewish people are encouraged from youngest years to "bless God" or praise God frequently during the day for the large and little gifts of the surrounding world. These include such diverse elements as water, sun, air, food, drink and caring relatives. Every created thing, therefore, can and should be acknowledged as a gift from God.

At Mass the Church follows a similar pattern, often blessing, praising and giving thanks to God for gifts received. For example, the priest recites quietly or aloud these prayers which obviously have their origin in the Jewish tradition:

Blessed are you, Lord, God of all creation.
Through your goodness we have this bread to offer,
which earth has given and human hands have made.
It will become for us the bread of life.

Blessed are you, Lord, God of all creation.
Through your goodness we have this wine to offer,
fruit of the vine and work of human hands.
It will become our spiritual drink.

In other official rituals, the Church, likewise, employs such created items as water, oil, bread and wine, the visible laying on of the hands and the pronouncement of spoken formulas as essential elements in those sacred rites.

The Church also provides blessings for things which people use in their everyday lives. These cover a variety of objects like a car, house, boat, field, seeds and animals, in addition to religious artifacts like candles, statues, medals, rosaries, crosses and crucifixes. Through these prayers we set the *blessed* item aside for a special task, acknowledge explicitly God's presence in all we do, and seek the Lord's help for the persons who will use the *blessed* object. The value or power of something *blessed* comes from the prayer of the person and the Church, not from the object itself.

The Church's **moral teaching** is another way it seeks to promote our earthly happiness through correct use of creation. *Nothing excessive* summarizes that approach, or *a proper balance,* or *The Middle Way.* Everything, according to these norms, is good or permissible as long as we use it in moderation.

For example, the Catholic Church does not prohibit its members from drinking alcoholic beverages. Yet it also teaches that immoderate consumption is wrong and could even become seriously sinful. Moreover, it praises the work of Alcoholics Anonymous and would urge persons with the disease of alcoholism to adopt that program of total abstinence.

However, the Church also understands the value of the ancient tradition of fasting and abstinence. The American bishops thus have encouraged Catholics to fast (limit the quantity of food and eliminate snacks) and abstain (refrain from eating meat) on Fridays as part of a spiritual effort to bring peace and justice into the world. In addition, the Church requires its constituents to fast and abstain on Ash Wednesday and Good Friday and to abstain during the Fridays of Lent.

Such fasting or abstaining, in essence, means temporarily foregoing a legitimate human pleasure intimately connected with life in order to sharpen our awareness that God and the life to come must have first priority within our hearts.

The Church, finally, wishing to help persons who are in any way hurting and to aid people seeking to improve their lives here on earth, fosters an enormous number of pastoral programs for those purposes. For example, an increasing percentage of parishes have established food pantries to feed the neighborhood hungry and bereavement committees to assist the grieving. Most parishes today provide enrichment sessions for parents who wish to have their babies baptized and marriage preparation programs for the engaged.

HAPPINESS HEREAFTER

We said that proper use of the created world around us can provide humans with relatively happy and joyful lives. *Relatively* is the key word.

Our experience shows that we do not live in a perfect world. Pleasures are never permanent; sickness, slight or serious, strikes all at some time. People hurt one another consciously or inadvertently. Natural disasters devastate areas with enormous destructive force. In addition, there is always the constant possibility of a sudden death and the certain fact of our eventual demise.

Various factors, therefore, can diminish our pleasure, dim our joys, or cloud our happiness. If we stay close to God, even those negative influences cannot rob us of a deep, inner peace. And the closer our relationship to God, the better we recognize the earthly beauty around us. Still, the fact remains that happiness here is imperfect and temporary.

In the face of this sobering reality the Church reminds us that perfect and permanent happiness must wait for the world of life beyond. In the letter to the Hebrews, for example, the writer states: *"For here we have no lasting city; we are seeking one which is to come."*[2]

At death, our body and spirit separate. The body almost immediately begins the deterioration which will return it to the dust from which it came. The spirit, on the other hand, indestructible and immortal, lives on and learns from God its destiny: eternal happiness in heaven, temporary purification in purgatory or an eternity in hell.

This book later examines heaven, purgatory and hell in detail. Here, however, we simply want to note that in our lasting city, in heaven, the quest for happiness will be over. All our desires will be fulfilled.

At every Mass the Church prays for those who have died. One of these prayers sketches a brief picture of the life to come, a snapshot of heaven based on the book of Revelation, chapter 21:

Welcome into your kingdom our departed brothers and sisters,
and all who have left this world in your friendship.
There we hope to share in your glory
When every tear will be wiped away.

On that day we shall see you, our God, as you are.
We shall become like you and praise you
forever through Christ our Lord,
from whom all good things come.

Both Franz Jaegerstaetter and St. Augustine searched earnestly for true happiness in their lives on earth. They ultimately found that this quest ended when they entered into a new and deeper relationship with God. Once these two holy men let the Lord govern their lives they discovered on the one hand how relatively joyful our existence here on earth can be. On the other hand, they recognized that permanent and perfect happiness must wait until after death when we enter a new world with God in heaven.

Welcome into your kingdom our departed brothers and sisters,
and all who have left this world in your friendship.
There we hope to share in your glory
When every tear will be wiped away.
On that day we shall see you, our God, as you are.
We shall become like you and praise you
forever through Christ our Lord,
from whom all good things come.

CHAPTER 3

Our Roots

THE CHALLENGE

My father left our home when I was two years old. Neither an older brother nor I ever discovered the critical causes of conflict between our parents or the actual reason for their divorce. Yet depart he did, remarried and, regrettably, died of cancer on a Christmas eve when I was only eight.

To her great credit, my mother never spoke poorly of dad. However, apparently he did not visit much after their breakup, because I have absolutely no picture in my memory of ever being with him.

His absence from both my life and memories rarely, if ever, seemed to be of concern to me until I crossed over into the thirties. Then gnawing questions began to arise: What was my father really like? Whom did I resemble most—mom or dad? How much of him is in me?

Subsequently, a casual but earnest quest for answers has gone on for the better part of over two decades. I have informally interrogated my brother and surviving relatives, read a piece about my father here or there, and even rescued a photo of this man who was half-responsible for my existence.

The need to uncover my roots obviously was, and is, a powerful drive inside of me.

THE RESPONSE

Alex Haley embarked upon a similar but much more difficult and devastating search for his past which he translated into the book and television series *Roots*. His story awakened within many Americans an interest in their own heritage, their own roots. This desire to trace our rootedness and to understand that we are part of an older, long-standing and even ancient tradition extends as well to our spiritual faith and religious practices.

11

TWENTY CENTURIES OLD

The Roman Catholic Church claims to be nearly two millenia old. It is a faith with Jewish roots, Jesus as its founder, Peter as its first leader and the present pope as Peter's successor in our day.

Visitors to Europe, and particularly Rome, quickly note numerous signs and buildings pointing to that belief in an unbroken religious tradition dating back to the time of Christ.

For example, at the Vatican, a tiny state within Italy, the famous St. Peter's basilica dominates the scene. Two statues on either side greet pilgrims as they approach this massive structure: Peter with two keys and Paul with a sword; Peter the preacher to the Jewish people and Paul the apostle to the Gentiles. Peter and Paul: the twin messengers of Jesus' gospel or good news.

Within the church itself, massive letters in Latin surrounding the dome carry these significant words of Jesus from Matthew 16: *"You are Peter and upon this rock I will build my Church . . . I will entrust to you the keys of the kingdom of heaven".* Beneath the letters and to the right of a huge altar is a statue of Peter, with the bronze protruding foot worn smooth by the touch of believing visitors over many years. Along a side corridor of the church is a list, carved on white marble, giving the succession of the 265 popes, beginning with Peter, Linus and Anacletus and continuing through to John XXIII, Paul VI and John Paul I.

Catholics accept the teaching that Christ established Peter as the initial leader of a Church that would carry on Jesus' message and mission until the end of time. The promise to Peter mentioned above was, according to this belief, fulfilled in John's gospel (Chapter 21) when the Risen Jesus says to him, *"Feed my lambs . . . Tend my sheep . . . Feed my sheep."* The prediction that Peter would be the rock foundation of the Church and its later fulfillment, were accompanied by assurances that *"the jaws of death shall not prevail against it."*

In other words, Christ will watch over his Church so that it will faithfully teach his message. This means that Christ has given the Church a unique power to communicate divine help to all its members and that he continues to protect the Church so it will never perish, despite weaknesses within and opposition without.

DIVINE AND HUMAN ELEMENTS

We could call those realities the mystery of the divine and human elements in the Church.

Catholics maintain that because of this divine element, the Church can never teach erroneously on matters of faith and morals. This is called *infallibility.* It is formally exercised only rarely by the Church. Catholics also recognize, however, that because of the human element in the Church, its leaders, members and history reflect the weaknesses and failures common to all women and men who have lived in this world.

Thus, some past popes, bishops, clergy and religious have led less than model lives. Nor has every lay person perfectly followed the teachings of the Church. Finally, all decisions by universal, national or local Church authorities have not been the most appropriate ones.

Still, despite its humanness the Catholic Church has survived, labeled by one American political leader as "the oldest enduring institution in the world." An English historian, not Roman Catholic, once uttered a famous comment that if any other human institution had known such great inner corruption or outer hostility, it would long ago have perished. For him the Catholic Church's very survival is almost proof of its divine protection.

Those faults and failures flowing out of that human element, nevertheless, have left their permanent scars. For instance, the effects of two major historical upheavals continue with us today.

13

Division In The East

A massive split developed between Catholics of the East centered around Constantinople and those of the West centered about Rome. Although it actually developed earlier, the year 1054 is looked at to mark the date when this division occurred. The Churches had been drifting apart through a process of isolation due to the theological, geographical and political forces. Tragic misunderstandings and human failures at that time led to conflicts seemingly out of proportion to the issues themselves. As a result, Patriarch Michael Cerularius of Constantinople and Cardinal Humbert, the papal legate, exchanged excommunications. The schism has not been healed to this day, but not since before the split have relations between the Churches of Rome and of Constantinople been as friendly as they are now. In fact, the excommunications of 1054 were officially lifted and "consigned to oblivion" by a joint declaration of Pope Paul IV and Patriarch Athenagoras I on December 7, 1965.

Attempts at reunion have met with varying success. From about 1500, a part of most of the Eastern churches made a reunion with Rome, so that today each tradition has as its heirs two Churches, one in union with the Church of Rome and one not in union. Those not in communion with Rome use the name "Orthodox," which means "of right belief."

The Churches of Rome and those in communion with it use the term "Catholic," which means "universal," as part of their name. The Marionite Catholic Church was never separated from the Roman Catholic Church and therefore has not gone through the process of division and reunion. While often referred to by Catholics as the "Eastern Rites," these churches are whole and complete Catholic Churches in communion with the Bishop of Rome and the Roman Catholic Church.

Reformation In The West

In the 16th century, the weaknesses of the Church's human element seemed to have gotten out of control. Scandalous lives, erroneous teachings and corrupt procedures were commonplace. Such things troubled some influential religious leaders of the day. People like Luther, Zwingli, Calvin, Hus and Knox sought to correct those abuses from within. However, the disagreement accelerated and intensified, culminating in a break away from the Catholic Church rather than a reform of the institution. People normally call this the Protestant (from "protest") Reformation, although the term Revolution might be more accurate, since, ultimately, these reformers rejected the pope's authority and started their own churches.

Those divisions rapidly multiplied Today the number of Protestant traditions which exist and the diversity of their beliefs and practices are enormous. Some are quite close to Roman Catholic teachings and procedures; others are very distant from them.

Serious efforts to promote understanding, to bridge painful gaps and to restore Christian unity began again in the 1950's and have produced many positive results. Still much remains to be done to effect a total healing of the multiple divisions among the Christian denominations.

Councils

To meet such inner challenges and external attacks, the Church, about every one hundred years, has summoned a *Council* of bishops from

around the world to deal with the current issues of the time, beginning with the Council of Jerusalem recorded in the Book of Acts, chapter 15.

For example, from 1545-1563 the Council of Trent examined those grievances which prompted the Protestant Reformation. As a result of this Council, the bishops issued a series of documents to clarify Catholic teachings. They also established a program of better education for the clergy, corrected and unified worship rituals, and revised institutional procedures. Called the Tridentine texts from the Latin word for Trent, those documents generally governed the Church's direction for the next four hundred years.

In 1962, an aging visionary and beloved pope, John XXIII, suddenly and surprisingly convened another Council, the 21st Ecumenical Council or Vatican Council II. Its purpose was not so much to correct problems in the Church as to renew or bring it up to date so that the Church might better meet the needs of our swiftly shifting society. Over 2,000 bishops from all over the globe assembled for Vatican II. They came together annually for four years and by means of the media their deliberations were made known instantly throughout the world. These bishops produced a series of impressive documents which have charted the course of the Catholic Church for the past two decades.

The directives of Vatican II have resulted in such developments as these: worship being in the vernacular, the language of the people, rather than in Latin; lay persons becoming more involved in almost every Church activity; and the Church publicly asserting a commitment to all human concerns, e.g., arms control, world hunger, family stability, civil rights.

The present pope, John Paul II, considers implementation of the Second Vatican Council to be one of his primary responsibilities. With remarkable energy, linguistic skills and personal charisma, he has captured world-wide attention by his frequent whirlwind journeys to every continent and his many forthright pronouncements on current issues.

However, the thrust of these messages is always the same. Very conscious of his role as successor to St. Peter and of the ancient tradition which he continues, Pope John Paul II seeks to proclaim with fidelity the good news of Jesus Christ. His words, though rooted in the past, are very much alive and have vital meaning for men and women of today.

CHAPTER 4

Words of Wisdom and Power

THE CHALLENGE

A priest traveled to New York some months back for an all day meeting at La Guardia airport. The sessions were tiresome and generally unproductive, leaving the participants at the end with weary bodies and downcast spirits.

As the priest rushed from the gathering room to catch a plane for the return home, he discovered to his dismay that a heavy fog had descended upon the airport forcing a delay and possible cancellation of all flights.

After a few hours of fruitless waiting for the mist to lift, the clergyman decided to stay overnight at a nearby motel and to try for an early morning departure.

Once settled into the motel, the priest looked around his room for something to read. He discovered a Gideon Bible in the desk drawer and skimmed through its pages until reaching a selection guide at the back of the volume.

The table offered suggestions of appropriate passages to meet a person's present moods and needs. Are you joyful? Read . . . Are you in pain? Read . . . Are you lonely? Read . . .

The priest, feeling rather down because of the day's developments, picked up on the last recommendation and flipped to the suggested psalm.

He skipped through the verses and at the end found someone had penned in this additional message:

"Are you still lonely? Call: 495- . . ."

THE RESPONSE

I am not sure whether this tale is truth or fiction, but the story invariably brings forth a chuckle. Yet it also touches upon real human situations and highlights our need for inspired words of guidance and strength, of wisdom and power during life's frequent confusing or discouraging moments.

The Catholic Church considers the Holy Bible as God's inspired word and recognizes the consequent wisdom and power in those biblical texts. Catholics are encouraged to read the Bible on a private, personal basis and the Church proclaims these scriptural words in a public community manner at every worship service.

THE BIBLE IN PUBLIC WORSHIP

On Sunday, for example, a male or female reader, often termed a lector, usually walks in the opening and concluding processions holding high a large, dignified and frequently decorated book. Called a lectionary, this volume is not a Bible, but rather a collection of excerpts from the biblical books arranged in systematic fashion covering a three year period.

Each weekend at every Mass, a reader proclaims two passages taken from either the Old Testament, the Acts of the Apostles, the New Testament letters or the book

of Revelation. Following these two Readings, the priest, or sometimes the deacon, will read a passage from the Gospels—the biblical narration which recounts the life of Jesus.

On solemn occasions, the lectern or pulpit where the Gospel is read

may have one or two candles nearby as a sign of the sacredness of the Gospel and a reminder that the message of Christ is a light to the world.

At the Second Vatican Council, the bishops decreed that the treasures of the Bible are to be opened up more lavishly, so that a richer fare may be provided for the faithful at the table of God's word. Today, over a three-year cycle, the scripture readings, read daily and at Sunday Mass, are drawn from nearly every book in the Bible.

THE BIBLE IN PERSONAL PRAYER

The Church today urges all its members to develop an enduring love for the Bible and to make the sacred scriptures central to their prayer lives. The bishops at Vatican Council II, for example, urged the Christian faithful *to learn the surpassing knowledge of Jesus Christ by frequent reading of the divine scriptures.* They cited, too, the words of St. Jerome, the famous 5th Century translator of the Bible, who said, *"Ignorance of the Scriptures is ignorance of Christ."*

At the time of the Reformation, the Church reacted strongly to the dissension caused by the various translations and interpretations of the Bible. As a result of that atmosphere, Catholics up until Vatican Council II, were not known as *Bi-*

ble people, and the scriptures received little attention in their personal lives.

This has radically changed in our day and practically every parish now has a Bible sharing group. Youngsters are usually provided with their own copy of the Bible, and many helps are offered for people who wish to read, pray and study the scripture.

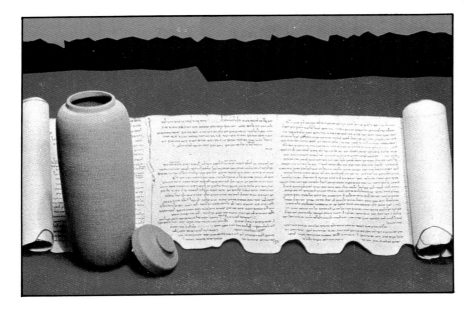

THE BIBLE'S DEVELOPMENT

There are, of course, two parts to the Bible: The Old Testament or Hebrew scriptures of 46 books and the New Testament collection of 27 books.

The Old Testament used by the apostles and early Christian Church was a Greek translation of the Hebrew scriptures called the Septuagint, prepared a few centuries before the time of Christ.

The New Testament developed slowly. The first Christians thought Jesus' second coming was imminent, so they were more concerned about preaching the life and message of Jesus rather than writing it down. Most of the writing was done in the second half of the first century, A.D. Moreover, these writings were not collected together as the New Testament for several generations. It was only by the end of the fourth century that the Church determined the present fixed "canon" or list of 27 books considered to be inspired.

All but one of these *canonical books* were written in the common Greek of the day. Jerome, a scholar of the fifth century, was asked by the Pope to translate each of the Old and New Testament books into Latin. His translation, known as the Vulgate (meaning "People's Language") edition, was used as the Church's official version until recent years.

When Latin ceased to be the common language of the people, the Church ultimately authorized translation into the vernacular. As a result, we now have many different versions of the Bible in a variety of languages. They are in essence the same, but with very distinguishing variations. Because of the advances in scholarship, we likewise possess today more translations which are closer to the original languages.

In earlier decades there seemed to be a difference between *Catholic and Protestant* Bibles. Some scholars had reservations about seven Old Testament books called the Apocrypha or deutero-canonical books: Tobit, Judith, Wisdom, Sirach (Ecclesiasticus), Baruch, 1 and 2 Maccabees, and parts of Daniel and Esther. In addition, Martin Luther rejected the New Testament books of Jude, Hebrews, James and Revelation. All of these were included in the Catholic Bible and excluded from certain Protestant Bibles. Those differences have generally disappeared today.

INSPIRED BY GOD

The Bible is not actually a single book, but rather a collection of books composed over a lengthy period of time. They are the works of many different authors with different styles of writing who produced their texts for a variety of purposes. Thus, to illustrate, there are books which contain poetry, prayer, songs, genealogies, history, prophesies, stories, exhortations as well as teachings about God and God's dealing with humankind.

The Church maintains that the entire Bible was written under divine inspiration. According to this belief, God is the principal author of the scriptures, influencing the human authors as they wrote, even though the writers composed freely and may not have been aware of this divine guidance. Because of such inspiration, we say that the authors wrote down the truths which God wished to reveal and in the way God wanted to reveal them.

However, each author wrote within the specific situation of her or his time and used a literary type, form or style best suited to the message. So if we wish to understand God's intended message, it is necessary to consider not only the literal sense of each text, but also its literary form and the author's cultural background.

TRADITION

As we have seen, the primitive Christian Church, at least until the end of the second century, spread almost totally through an oral rather than a written process; through spoken, handed-down beliefs rather than through the printed books of the Bible.

Moreover, as certain New Testament letters even state, some of the biblical writings are difficult to comprehend, requiring commentary, explanation or interpretation. Important as the Bible is to us, it is not an exhaustive handbook of the Christian faith nor a neat package of clearly defined truths. Our understanding of Christian beliefs has developed over the years and continues to unfold throughout the Church's history.

That spoken, living process of handing down the teachings of Christianity is known as Tradition. While the seed or core of all beliefs can be found in the scriptures, the Bible does not stand alone but requires the Church's tradition for its full impact to be realized. The Church is continually explaining and unfolding the truths of our faith as Jesus gave them to us.

We discover this tradition from a variety of sources: the creeds we recite, the way we worship, the writings of scholars and Church leaders, the decrees of popes and councils, the prayers of Christians and the universal sense of judgments of Church members. The Church, nevertheless, gives special value to the tradition expressed in the very early Church because of its closeness to the time of Jesus. It, therefore, examines carefully the writings and practices of the Church in the first centuries after Christ.

A PEOPLE OF THE WORD

Catholic Trappist monks at the Abbey of Genesee near Rochester, New York, like other Trappists in monasteries in the world, rise at 2:00 a.m. and chant the Liturgy of the Hours, a collection of mostly biblical songs, prayers and readings. They then spend perhaps an hour or more in private, individual divine reading of the scriptures, a time for prayerful pondering of the Bible.

Far south of this New York abbey, in Jacksonville, Florida, Francis and Barbara Scholtz start each morning by meditating at home on the scriptural passages for that day's Mass. Later, at meetings, Francis begins working sessions by pulling a small New Testament from his pocket and reading an appropriate excerpt.

Both groups of people, though in quite different ways, find in the Bible words of wisdom and power for their lives.

CHAPTER 5

Heroes/ Heroines

THE CHALLENGE

The Missionaries of Charity, Mother Teresa of Calcutta's community of sisters, rise before dawn. They spend an hour or more at private prayer and public Mass, work throughout the day with the poorest of the world's poor, and at night return to the chapel for another hour of adoration of the Lord in the Blessed Sacrament.

Not everyone knows about those long periods of prayer, but most people do know Mother Teresa and her sisters dressed in their simple but distinctive blue and white Indian garb. They also know the kind of work these nuns undertake— serving persons with AIDS, comforting the lepers, caring for the dying, accepting abandoned babies, and, in general, helping those whom no one else will or can assist.

When a visitor to Calcutta asked the elderly foundress of this community why she and her sisters engage in such difficult tasks, the Nobel prize winner looked about a room crowded with desperately afflicted individuals and simply said, "This is Jesus in his distressing disguises."

On one occasion, a young sister was kneeling beside a dying man, gently caring for his needs and quite oblivious of those around her. A visitor stood at a distance watching this scene for some time, then turned and walked out.

As he passed by Mother Teresa, the man remarked, "Mother, when I came here this afternoon I was bitter, angry with God and about to give up my faith. But I discovered the Lord's presence in that young nun and I am leaving in great peace, with my faith rekindled."

THE RESPONSE

This tormented man discovered a heroine, someone whom he could look up to and be inspired by, during his days of darkness. The remarkable number of young women who today have left the comfort of home to enter the Missionaries of Charity have likewise found in Mother Teresa a human heroine worth imitating. But she would caution her followers to look instead to her own hero, Jesus Christ, whom she finds in the poorest of the poor.

JESUS CHRIST

It seems we all hunger for models. For Catholics, Jesus Christ is the hero—a person who is Son of God and son of Mary, who walked on the water and yet wept for a friend. Jesus is both divine and human, perfect in all respects, while still like us in every way except sin.

Sunday after Sunday, Catholics express their beliefs about Jesus Christ, this hero and model, with these phrases of the Profession of Faith or Nicene Creed:

. . . We believe in one Lord, Jesus Christ
the only Son of God,
eternally begotten of the Father
God from God, Light from Light,
true God from true God,
begotten, not made, one in Being with the Father.
Through him all things were made.
For us and for our salvation
he came down from heaven:

by the power of the Holy Spirit
he was born of the Virgin Mary, and became man.

For our sake he was crucified under Pontius Pilate;
he suffered, died, and was buried.
On the third day he rose again
in fulfillment of the Scriptures;
he ascended into heaven
and is seated at the right hand of the Father.
He will come again in glory
to judge the living and the dead,
and his kingdom will have no end. . . .

Since the Church views itself as the Risen Jesus in our midst today, carrying on his work of preaching, guiding and saving, it is dedicated to making known Christ's life and teachings to everyone.

From our own earliest years until our death, the Church guides us in the ways of Jesus. Parents preparing for the baptism of infants, pre-schoolers in the programs on Sundays, and students from Catholic institutions as well as the public school system learn the message of Jesus in their religion classes. Adults, too, participate in many types of adult religious education programs. Finally, those in mourning for a deceased loved one hear from the Church about the promise of new life given to us by Jesus.

THE CHURCH YEAR

But the Church over the centuries has developed a unique method for annually re-presenting in a vital way the entire life of Jesus Christ. Known as the Church year, it celebrates various events related to the Savior on certain specified Sundays and other days during the year.

The central feast of the Church is Easter Sunday, just as it was in ancient times. The Church relives on this day the Resurrection of the Lord, his victory over sin, darkness and death. This event is the rock foundation of the Christian faith and, naturally, it became the foundation stone of the Church Year.

As the Church developed, additional aspects of Christ's life came to be singled out and celebrated with special feasts or seasons.

For example, at Christmas we relive his birth and entrance into the world. During Lent we walk with him through his forty days of prayer and fasting. On Palm Sunday we commemorate his short-lived, king-like entrance into Jerusalem. Within Holy Week we recall his last meal or supper in the Upper Room, his agony on the cross and his three days buried in the tomb. Forty days after his resurrection, on Ascension Thursday, we watch as Jesus "ascends" to the Father, and on Pentecost we re-experience the outpouring of the Holy Spirit upon the apostles.

The Church teaches that these worship celebrations are not mere historical re-creations but have unique blessings or graces connected with them for those who participate in an active, faith-filled manner.

VESTMENT COLORS

As a particular way of symbolizing events in the year, the Church uses different colors for the vestments and altar decorations. Purple indicates a time of expectation, purification or penance. White or gold expresses joy and triumph. Red is a sign of royalty, fire and martyrdom; green, of life and growth.

The following simplified table of highlights of the Church Year may help clarify its meaning:

Season or Feast	Time & Meaning	Liturgical Color
Advent	Four weeks of preparation for Christ's coming on December 25	Purple
Christmas-Epiphany	Christ's birth and early manifestation	White
Lent	40 days of penitential preparation for baptism and Easter	Purple
Easter	Christ's Resurrection and the Risen Lord's appearance to his followers	White
Pentecost	Descent of the Holy Spirit (Acts 2)	Red
Ordinary Time	The Church hearing and living Jesus' message	Green

SAINTS

The Church, recognizing that Christ is the only mediator between God and us, urges all to keep eyes fixed on him alone. Still it does propose for our inspiration and help people from the past who have walked closely in Jesus' footsteps.

We call them saints and believe that they have reached heaven, our ultimate goal. Moreover, the Church through its teaching about the Communion of Saints maintains that these women and men can assist us by their prayers before God.

MARY

At the top of the list is Mary, the mother of Jesus. From the earliest days, the Church has consistently given special honor to this woman often called *Our Lady*. Quite succinctly, the Church states that since she is Christ's mother and since Jesus is God, then Mary can rightfully be called the Mother of God.

Although a creature and human like us, the Church teaches that she was particularly blessed or graced by God in many ways. Mary was conceived without original sin. Mary remained a virgin before, during, and after the birth of Christ. During her life she did not sin. Finally, she was assumed or taken body and spirit into heaven

Catholics commonly pray to Mary or, more accurately, through this woman to Christ, her son. We ask her to speak for us, intercede for us with Jesus, much after the fashion that we might plead with a human mother to intervene on our behalf with her child. The famous *Ave Maria*, or Hail Mary, expresses this notion in words taken almost entirely from the gospel of Luke:

Hail Mary, full of grace
The Lord is with you.
Blessed are you among women
And blessed is the fruit of your
womb, Jesus.
Holy Mary, Mother of God,
Pray for us sinners
Now and at the hour of our death.

The rosary is a very popular method of prayer used by Catholics when they wish to honor Mary and ask for her assistance. A prayer tradition over a thousand years old, it consists of a crucifix and series of connected beads upon which a person recites in repetitive fashion the *Creed, Lord's Prayer, Hail Mary,* and *Glory be to the Father, Son and Holy Spirit.*

OTHER SAINTS

In every century, culture and continent there have been followers of Christ who made the imitation of Jesus their first priority. These include such people as the twelve

Apostles in the first century, St. Francis of Assisi and St. Clare in the middle ages, St. Elizabeth Bayley Seton and St. John Neumann in contemporary times.

Catholics look upon these Christian heroes as inspirational models, often naming children after them. Since such saints are God's special friends, they are considered intercessors with God. Catholics do not pray *to,* but *through* these acknowledged holy men and women *to God* for assistance.

The Church Year incorporates officially declared saints into its annual schedule of celebrations. Unlike most feasts of Christ, however, observances for Mary and the other saints occur on fixed days every year. There are thirteen different feasts honoring Mary (e.g., the Immaculate Conception—December 8, the Assumption—August 15), but the other saints have a single feast day (e.g., St. Thomas the Apostle—July 3, St. Francis of Assisi—October 4; Mother Seton—January 4).

The Church in our time examines very thoroughly the life of a deceased person before acclaiming her or him a saint. If that study reveals a heroic degree of holiness in the in-

dividual's life and if verifiable miracles are credited to the candidate, the Church officially declares in solemn ceremony that she or he is with God in heaven.

Following faithfully in the footsteps of Jesus Christ is an on-going lifelong challenge. He, indeed, is our perfect hero, but we also need other lesser heroes to encourage us on this long journey of faith. The Church Year fulfills that necessity by keeping both the mysteries of Jesus and the examples of saints constantly before our eyes.

The Challenge

CHAPTER 6

Talking with God

Visitors to New York City almost automatically list Radio City Music Hall, the United Nations and the now refurbished Statue of Liberty as places of note to explore.

But many, including people of quite diverse religious affiliations, would also stop at St. Patrick's Cathedral and wander through the spacious church.

George Spielman was no exception. As a leader of the Family Life Education office for a Catholic diocese in Missouri, he had been invited to the Big Apple to participate in a teleconference on marriage preparation. During free hours before the program and after the program, George, like many tourists, took a guided bus trip about the city and eventually entered St. Patrick's for a visit.

He discovered inside both a constant flow of people and yet a very subdued environment. Individuals or groups slowly walked about the interior, marveling at its beauty, while others remained in the pews, praying in reflective silence.

During the early morning hours, at noon, and toward evening, the crowd of praying people grew significantly. They were mostly Catholics who gathered for weekday Masses celebrated at those times.

Outside of Mass times, however, those who prayed did so in a variety of ways. Some held rosary beads in their fingers; others moved along the stations of the cross; still others read from devotional books. Many sat or knelt, quietly speaking with God about matters of concern in words known only to them and their Maker. A few stood before candle stands, dropped in coins, lit tapers, prayed momentarily and walked on.

Spielman closely observed all of this. He was not raised a Roman Catholic but became one in his adult years. As a result, some of the Church's traditional devotions that he noted in this cathedral seemed foreign, even awkward for him. But the massive church and awesome atmosphere seemed to touch him. He returned to the vestibule and told his campanions, "I just did something for the first time in my life. I lit a candle in church."

The Response

It would be interesting to know what all those people, including George Spielman, were praying about. It seems that they must have been talking over with God matters of great personal importance to them.

Was one giving thanks for a new job, restored health or a family reconciliation? Was another overwhelmed with guilt and seeking forgiveness? Was this person worried about the future and needing reassurance? Was that individual, crushed by recent bad news, asking for wisdom to understand or strength to bear a burden?

Prayer

The fact is that every human being has those kinds of inner needs or anxieties. People who are believers tend to take such concerns to God. That communication or talking with our Creator we call prayer: a friend speaking with a friend in a conversation which often is about a friend or friends. Sometimes, however, the period of prayer is less a conversation and more like two lovers simply being present to each other.

The Catholic Church may appear rigid to some with its supposedly strict rules governing the devotion of its members. In truth, however, regulations concerning the prayer life of Catholics is minimal. Many opportunities and alternatives are offered; very little is obligatory.

Minimal Obligations

For example, parishes generally provide at least one Mass each day, but attendance at the Eucharist is obligatory only on Sundays and in the United States on the following six "holy days of obligation":

Feast	Date
Feast of Mary's Immaculate Conception	December 8
Christmas	December 25
Octave of Christmas, Solemnity of Mary, Mother of God	January 1
Ascension Thursday	(40 days after Easter)
Feast of Mary's Assumption	August 15
All Saint's Day	November 1

The Eucharist is celebrated on a daily basis, but Catholics are required to receive the Lord under the sign of the consecrated bread and wine only once annually. This *Easter duty* may be fulfilled during the three-month period between Ash Wednesday and Trinity Sunday. The Church encourages members to approach Communion frequently, even daily; therefore, the *Easter duty* — legislated long ago in an era of popular piety that discouraged reception of the Eucharist because of our unworthiness — is a minimal obligation.

On the other hand, the Catholic Church offers for its members a rich array of prayer forms or styles from which to choose. Some of these possibilities are public or communal and others are personal or individual.

PUBLIC PRAYER

The Church's official public prayer or worship is called the liturgy, a term derived from a Greek word signifying some public work to be performed by the citizens of the state. In liturgical prayer, members of the Church gather together and worship in a formal way according to approved rules and texts. In this format, the assembled community, after speaking as a body to God the Father through Jesus Christ in the Holy Spirit, listens in response then presents offerings to the Creator and receives gifts in return. The liturgy is considered the summit toward which every Church activity is directed as well as the source from which all its power flows.

There are several distinct liturgical rites: The Mass, the center of Catholic worship; the seven sacraments; the Liturgy of the Hours mentioned in the fourth chapter; the Church year also described earlier; certain formal devotions; and a collection of blessings for most of the objects and activities which are part of everyday life.

THE MASS

The name *Mass* developed centuries ago from a Latin word in the concluding dismissal rite. The term meant *sent* and the Latin phrase, *Ite, missa est* conveyed the notion of *Go, it is finished. You are being sent out now. Carry over what you have heard and received into your daily lives.* Eventually the entire celebration came to be known as the *Missa* or *Mass* in English. We see remnants of this in one of the optional conclusions to our present service: *The Mass is ended, go in peace.*

The Mass is also called a Eucharist or Eucharistic Celebration. Eucharist originates from a Greek word which means *giving thanks,* a phrase that appears in the New Testament accounts of the Last Supper. Since Catholics view the Mass as the re-presentation of the Last Supper and the idea of *giving thanks* repeatedly occurs in it, we frequently speak about the Mass as a Eucharist or Eucharistic Celebration.

The Mass is also referred to as the Holy Sacrifice or the Sacrifice of the Mass, because Catholic teaching maintains that through this liturgical event, the sacrifice of Jesus on the cross is perpetuated in an unbloody manner.

Every Mass has four basic parts or sections:

1. A relatively brief gathering rite which seeks to create a prayerful community.

2. A Liturgy of the Word which takes place at a lectern or pulpit. It consists of scriptural readings plus a sermon or homily with various sung or spoken responses by the people.

3. A Liturgy of the Eucharist which centers around the altar. It consists of preparing the gifts of bread and wine, consecrating them into the body and blood of Jesus and distributing the blessed particles to the participants.

4. A short dismissal ritual which sends refreshed believers out to transform the world.

Mass is celebrated today according to official rules and books published in 1970. This relatively new format, the first major revision in 400 years, features within it a diversity of prayerful activities and leadership roles.

29

PEOPLE PARTICIPATION

Participants at Mass alternately stand out of respect or praise, kneel in adoration or repentance, or sit in attentiveness or reflection. They also respond together in word or song, exchange a greeting of peace, and spend moments in silence.

A priest presides over the celebration, but according to the revised directives he is assisted by a variety of liturgical "ministers." These persons, generally lay people of the parish, are trained and commissioned for their tasks. They serve as greeters to welcome worshipers, ushers, scripture readers, leaders of song, choir members, servers around the altar and distributors of Communion.

While individual, personal involvement is necessary at the Mass, still the emphasis at a Eucharist is on the communal, public dimension of worship. As a united body or community of believers, we both praise God and hear God's Word, offer our gifts and lives to God and receive Jesus' body and his blood in return.

The different elements of public prayer sketched here for the Mass will be found as well in other liturgical celebrations.

PERSONAL PRAYER

But the Church likewise provides an enormously rich range of alternatives for personal, individualized prayer. These are totally optional. Every Catholic is free to choose whatever style of prayer is comfortable and to use that, or another form whenever desirable.

Here are a few samples of individual approaches to prayer frequently used by Catholics today.

*FORMAL PRAYERS

Individuals or groups may recite silently or aloud traditional prayer formulas that are rooted in the scriptures, for example, the Our Father and the Hail Mary. Other commonly recited prayers have been developed by the Church (e.g. the Creed or the Act of Contrition) and some have come from the pen of religious leaders like the well known Prayer of St. Francis.

*INFORMAL PRAYING

Catholics have always talked quietly with God in their own words and that pattern continues. However, young people today are taught more directly how to pray in this way not only privately, but also with others, especially at meal time and before meetings or with a small group of like-minded persons.

*RELIGIOUS STATUES, PICTURES, MEDALS

These are meant to help represent for the believer Jesus, Mary, or some saint. Catholics never pray to these items in themselves, which would be idolatry, but cherish them as reminders of God's presence and of those whose lives were dedicated to God.

*STATIONS OF THE CROSS

A Catholic church normally has erected along the walls 14 images which depict the journey of Jesus from his condemnation by Pilate until his burial in the tomb. Individuals or groups pray silently or with prepared texts as they move from one station to another and traditionally recite, "We adore you, O Christ, and we bless you, because by your holy cross you have redeemed the world."

*ROSARY

This popular devotion, explained in the previous chapter, is also prayed quietly and privately or sometimes publicly and vocally.

*NOVENAS

The early followers of Jesus prayed in expectation for nine days after Christ's ascension into heaven. They were pleading for the promised coming of the Holy Spirit. The biblical event has spawned innumerable other nine-day patterns of prayer centered on a particular intention. The word novena, from the Latin root meaning "nine," emerged to describe these phenomena.

*THE BIBLE

Since the Second Vatican Council, Catholics have become increasingly "bible-oriented" people. They generally possess their own copies of the scripture and use them as a source for individual or group prayer.

*CHARISMATICS

Over the past two decades many Catholics have also become involved in approved charismatic prayer groups which include in their meetings spontaneous vocal prayers, praying or singing in tongues, constant reference to the scriptures, testimonies, prophecies and great emphasis on a personal relationship with Jesus and an openness to the Holy Spirit.

*DEVOTIONAL CANDLES

Most Catholic Churches continue to maintain some type of arrangement by which individuals can light a candle before an altar or statue. The gesture is a sort of tribute to the Lord, his mother or a saint. It is also a way of stating in a visible way the wish that the prayer offered in church will continue on after the in-

dividual leaves the building and goes about her or his daily duties.

There are other ways of personal and public prayer, but these are the most commonly encountered prayer forms within the Catholic Community.

THE CHALLENGE

Faith

Charles de Foucald was left an orphan in France at a very young age, but a caring grandfather assumed responsibility for the child and fostered in him a devotion to family, country and God. He also developed in the lad a great love for reading, serious study and silence.

Although raised as a Catholic, Charles, soon after high school, lost his faith, largely through doubts caused by extensive reading of the works of irreligious and skeptical writers.

The absence of faith left a void within him, and Foucald turned to various pleasures for relief, comfort and reassurance. "He spent money lavishly and wildly. He gambled, drank and ate without restraint. He entertained on a grand scale. He was overweight and overdressed. He entered into an alliance with a young woman." In short, Charles became an "aimless, purposeless young man."

However, during travels to Africa in the midst of this turmoil, he encountered some Jews. He envied their belief in God which had survived all kinds of suffering and persecution. On this same continent, he was struck by the simple, direct faith of Moslems and their practice of kneeling five times each day and facing Mecca to pray.

Eventually, Charles de Foucald spiritually hit rock bottom. At that low point he returned to God, confessing to a priest in Paris.

However, his faith still remained unsteady and weak. This prompted him to spend long hours every day in a church, kneeling and repeating what he termed his "strange prayer": *My God, if you exist, make your presence known to me.*

God did and Charles de Foucald went on to give his life in prayer, writing and service for tribes in the African desert. Ultimately, he was murdered by a hostile group on December 1, 1916. Today thousands around the world follow his teachings and imitate his example.[1]

THE RESPONSE

Faith and prayer are interconnected. People pray because they believe there is Someone beyond who hears them and can respond. Therefore, faith is the foundation for all prayer.

But people also pray to have their faith strengthened. The apostles once quite simply asked of Jesus, *"Increase our faith." (Luke 17:5)* Charles de Foucald was making the same request during those long hours at prayer in that parish church.

Prayer, therefore, presupposes faith but likewise deepens it. The term *"faith,"* however, generally possesses two meanings: it can refer to a body of truths which we accept or to a power which enables us to accept those truths.

For example, a book explaining the teachings of Catholicism carries this sub-title:*"A Modern Presentation of the Catholic Faith."* The word *faith* in that usage obviously means those truths which Catholics endorse. On the other hand, when we state that Charles de Foucald lost or regained his faith, the word *faith* in such a context means the inner ability or power which enabled him to espouse the Church's teachings.

FAITH AS A BODY OF TRUTHS

At the end of John's gospel, the author mentions: *"There are still many other things that Jesus did, yet if they were written about in detail, I doubt there would be room enough in the entire world to hold the books to record them."*
(John 21:25)

We could almost make a similar statement about the teachings of the Catholic Church. As an illustration of that point, two current texts attempt merely to outline the basic tenets of Catholicism. One requires over 400, and the other almost 300 pages to do so.

However, from the beginning of Christianity until the present moment, there has been need for succinct formulas which clearly summarize the major beliefs of the Church. We name these formulas "creeds" from the Latin word *credo* meaning, *I believe.*

Most Catholics in the past memorized the Apostles' Creed, a credal statement dating back to the first years of Christianity. The name comes from the time of its origin—the Apostolic period— rather than from its being the work of one or all of the twelve apostles. The Apostles' Creed cited below expresses in a brief and simple way the main articles of the Catholic faith.

I believe in God, the Father Almighty, Creator of heaven and earth, and in Jesus Christ his only Son Our Lord, who was conceived by the Holy Spirit, born of the Virgin Mary, suffered under Pontius Pilate, was crucified, died and was buried. He descended into hell, the third day he rose again from the dead; he ascended into heaven, and sits at the right hand of God the Father Almighty. From thence he shall come to judge the living and the dead. I believe in the Holy Spirit, the Holy Catholic Church, the Communion of Saints, the forgiveness of sins, the resurrection of the body, and life everlasting. Amen.

At different stages in the Church's history, the necessity of expanding upon the Apostles' Creed and developing a new formula to meet certain specific challenges became clear to Church leaders. At the Council of Nicea in 325 A.D., for example, the assembled bishops produced an expression of faith called the Nicene Creed which responded to attacks being made then upon the divinity of Christ. Eventually, the Church made this the standard profession of faith recited or sung in Latin at Sunday Masses.

Pope Paul VI (1963-1978), following that long tradition of the Church, published a Credo which emphasized several additional items about the faith that are of particular concern in our century.

These three creeds and other similar credal statements explicitly mention several articles of the faith, but they implicitly contain all of the truths that the Church teaches.

FAITH AS AN INNER POWER

There are extraordinary sunrises and sunsets in the desert areas which surround Tuscon, Arizona. On a quiet evening two persons stand side by side, both in awe of the spectacular beauty before them. One comments on the magnificence of the scene; the other praises the Lord for it. One does not move past the external sight, the other looks beyond it to God the creator. The latter response requires faith; the former does not.

Thus we can also consider or define faith as that which enables us to look beyond, an inner power which opens doors and helps us see something more. The believer not only appreciates nature's beauties, but discovers beyond them a wise, powerful and caring God manifested through this splendid creation.

The believer, burdened by a fatal disease, personal tragedy or family crisis, is open to the event not merely as a problem to be solved, but more as a mystery to be experienced. Moreover, the believer sees a loving God always present in these dark moments, sustaining those afflicted and ultimately bringing good out of the bad.

The believer likewise views death as a beginning, not an end; a comma, not a period; a change to something better, not the end of all life's joys.

In their document on the liturgy, the bishops at the Second Vatican Council taught that *"Christ is always present in his Church, especially in her liturgical celebrations."* (Article 7) The bishops enumerated the various presences of Jesus in the Liturgy. The Church, wishing to dramatize Christ's presence in these diverse ways, surrounds them with rich signs and symbols. Those actions and objects help stir up the faith of believers and make it easier for them to see in life's experiences the presence and promise of the Risen Savior.

These are a few of the ways, mentioned by the Council document, that the Lord is present in our liturgical celebrations:

1. In the sacrifice of the Mass, Christ is present in the person of his minister. The same Jesus who formerly offered himself on the cross now offers himself through the ministry of his priests.

The priest presiding at the Eucharist wears special vestments, indicating the uniqueness of his role as leader of worship. Originally the priest wore the ordinary garb of the Roman world. With the influx of barbarians and a consequent shift in the style of clothing, the church retained for the priest the garments of the earlier centuries. The tendency in the Middle Ages to give symbolic religious meaning to nearly every action or object carried over to the priest's vestments. The garments worn at Mass today, therefore, trace their origin to the basic clothing of early Romans with later adaptions and added symbolism.

2. Christ is present in Holy Communion. Catholics believe that under the sign of the bread and wine, the Risen Jesus is truly and substantially present. Priests, deacons or carefully trained eucharistic ministers present the consecrated bread or wine with the words, *Body of Christ* or *Blood of Christ.* The communicant responds, *Amen,* which in effect is an act of faith saying, *That is true,* or *I believe it* or *Yes.* Whether the recipient immediately receives the blessed particle on the hand or on the tongue, the Church urges at this moment an inner attitude and visible expression of reverence.

3. Christ is present in the reserved sacrament. Originally, the consecrated elements, especially the blessed bread, were reserved simply for later distribution to the sick or prisoners and for self-communication

during the week when there was no daily Mass. Later in Medieval days, Catholics developed a devotion to this Real Presence reserved in a safe, locked compartment called a tabernacle, a practice which continues today.

Church law requires that chapels containing the reserved eucharist maintain a constantly burning sanctuary lamp or tabernacle candle.

4. Christ is present in the sacraments. Thus, by Jesus' power when anybody baptizes, it is really Christ himself who baptizes; when a couple marry each other, it is really Christ who marries them; when a priest absolves from sin or anoints the sick, it is really Christ who forgives and heals. *We will explore some of the surrounding signs and symbols of the sacraments in the chapters which follow.*

5. Christ is present in the scriptures proclaimed at the Liturgy. As the bishops of the Church state,"*He is present in the Word since it is he himself who speaks when the holy scriptures are read in church.*"

We have already seen how the Church emphasizes this presence by having specially prepared lectors or readers proclaim the text, by using a dignified, decorated volume for this proclamation and by encouraging candles, processions and incense at the gospel. In addition, both the proclaimer of the gospel and the people make a tiny cross with the right thumb on their foreheads, lips and hearts at the introduction. This manifests a hope that they may understand these words with their minds, express them during their conversations and believe them in their hearts. At the end of the gospel, the priest or deacon elevates the book and declares, *"This is the gospel of the Lord,"* while the congregation responds, *"Praise to you, Lord Jesus Christ."*

6. Christ is present when the Church prays and sings. The Council Fathers recall Jesus' promise in the gospel, "*When two or three are gathered together in my name, there am I in the midst of them.*" (Matthew 18:20)

Roman Catholics, prior to the Second Vatican Council, tended to be non-singing, silent spectators at worship events, especially the Mass. The revised rituals and principles of worship seek to change that pattern. Those present are encouraged to be active participants in the word, song and deed. While most Catholics have not yet become known as enthusiastic singers at worship, still in almost every church visitors will find hymnals or pamphlets called missalettes in the seats. These contain suitable music for congregational participation. Moreover, a variety of choirs and musical styles, together with song leaders for the congregation, have become commonplace in Catholic parishes.

THE GIFT OF FAITH

Charles de Foucald received faith as a free gift in his childhood years, lost it, but then regained the power to believe as a gift from God. This remains perhaps the greatest mystery of all: faith—the power to recognize the divine presence in our midst and accept it—is a totally free, absolutely unearned gift from God. Like Charles de Foucald, if we never have possessed faith, if our faith wavers, if our faith has vanished, we have no alternative but to say,"*My God, make your presence known to me* or *Lord, increase my faith.*"

CHAPTER 8

The Need to Belong

there with giant tears rolling down his cheeks and his shoulders violently heaving.

Not very skilled at comforting lonely seven-year-olds, I reluctantly moved over by the sobbing boy. We talked a bit (in short sentences) and I learned that his name was Jason and that his single parent mother had put him on this plane to Dallas for a visit to his grandmother.

What does a fifty-year old celibate do in such circumstances?

Breakfast came and that helped pass about ten minutes. I tucked a napkin under his chin and he spread butter all over the roll, I cut his meat and he saturated the ham with salt. I obtained some orange juice for him and he picked at the potatoes. With the meal over, I found a magazine and read one story about a Ranger Rick to him. Fortunately for me, Jason soon fell asleep and I returned to my original seat.

An hour later the plane landed at O'Hare.

I moved over next to Jason and informed him, *"Here is where I must get off, Jason. But like your mother said, before lunch you will be in Dallas, your grandmother will be waiting for you, and everything will be fine."*

My great reassurance didn't work. For the boy looked up to me with the saddest of eyes and pleaded, *"But who is going to take care of me now?"*

THE RESPONSE

In less than two hours, the plane would land in Texas where Jason would run out of the aircraft, jump into his grandmother's arms and hold on tight. He would regain his sense of belonging to someone.

THE CHALLENGE

I had just settled into my spot along the aisle on an American Airlines 7:00 flight to Chicago when the attendant interrupted me and guided a young boy over to the window seat in my section. Once he was situated, I rebuckled, returned to my prayer book and became absorbed in the text.

As the plane eventually raced down the runway on the takeoff, I was shaken out of my silent preoccupation by the sound of sobs. Separated from me by the center seat, my youthful co-traveler sat

37

But on that American Airlines flight, during those moments of the takeoff and of my departure, he felt alone, isolated, unloved and belonging to no one.

In theory and ideal, every Catholic who walks into church for a weekend Mass should feel like Jason did when he left the plane and was caught up in his grandmother's embrace: welcomed and loved. In fact and practice, many Catholics or visitors to our churches may feel more like Jason did while he was on the plane: alone and isolated.

According to both theory and ideal, each Catholic does belong and should feel that way at worship. In point of fact and practice, some Catholics often do not have a sense that they belong and do not feel welcome.

THE HORIZONTAL OR COMMUNITY DIMENSION

The model for a Catholic parish or community, both in the way it lives and the way it worships, has already been sketched for believers in the Acts of the Apostles. This excerpt from the second chapter illustrates the life of the early Christian communities:

They devoted themselves to the apostles' instruction and the communal life, to the breaking of the bread and the prayers. A reverent fear overtook them all, for many wonders and signs were performed by the apostles. Those who believed shared all things in common; they would sell their property and goods, dividing everything on the basis of each one's need. They went to the temple area together every day, while in their homes they broke the bread. With exultant and sincere hearts they took their meals in common, praising God and win-

ning the approval of all the people. Day by day the Lord added to their number those who were being saved.

The Church in official teachings about its nature and its formal regulations about the way members should worship affirms that model from apostolic days. Whether we look to the image of the Church as the Mystical Body of Christ which Pope Pius XII stressed in the 1940's or the Church as the People of God which the Second Vatican Council emphasized in the 1960's, the basic notion remains the same.

The Catholic Church views itself as a community of believers, a group of women and men linked together by a common bond of faith, grace and baptism; a body of persons who share the same life and beliefs.

It follows logically from this understanding of the Church's nature that members ought to be one in heart and mind, living in uni-

ty and caring for one another. The New Testament letters from John, Paul and others proclaimed as the second reading at Sunday Masses, constantly recall that ideal.

■

"Make every effort to preserve the unity which has the Spirit as its origin. . . Live a life worthy of the calling you have received. . . bearing with one another lovingly." (Ephesians 4:1-3)

■

"Make my joy complete by your unanimity, possessing the one love, united in the spirit and ideals." (Philippians 2:2)

■

"Bear with one another. . . over all these virtues put on love, which binds the rest together and makes them perfect." (Colossians 3:13-14)

■

"This, remember, is the message you heard from the beginning: We should love one another." (John 3:11).

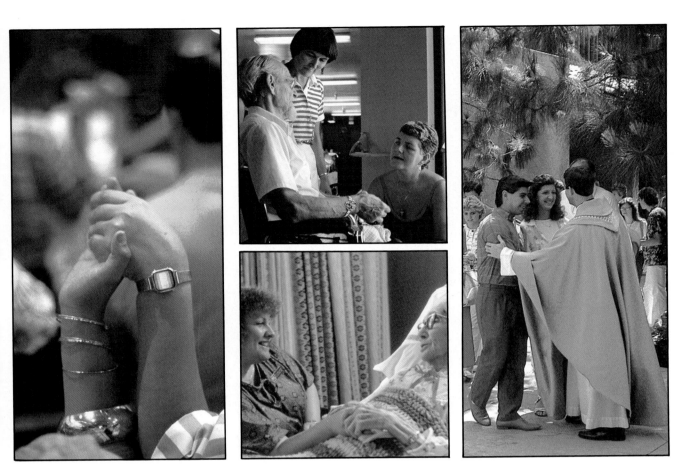

The Bishops at Vatican II underscored in the Liturgy Constitution that worship services are not private functions but celebrations of the church. Therefore, they emphasize that whenever possible, rites should be celebrated in common, not in a semi-private manner. People should be present and actively participating.

COMMUNITY BUILDING EFFORTS

All of the ritual books published since the Second Vatican Council explicitly call for that community dimension of worship with specific directions about congregational participation. Parishes have been quite faithful to the task of implementing those regulations and have also invented creative ways of enhancing the communal aspect of parish life and worship:

*Some of the sacraments, notably Baptism, Confirmation and Anointing, are occasionally celebrated within a Sunday Mass to demonstrate their relationship to the whole community. For example, Baptism is a welcoming into the total church, the entire Christian community, symbolized by those present for the particular weekend Eucharist. Or Anointing within the eucharistic celebration dramatizes the entire Church praying and caring for the sick.

*Churches have been built or renovated to provide seating arrangements that allow a better physical and visual exchange between participants, thus enhancing the community spirit.

*More and more parishes have *greeters* or *ministers of hospitality*, volunteers from the parish who welcome people to worship, sometimes even seating guests and introducing them.

*A few parishes have books for visitors to sign and letters are sent to them afterwards, acknowledging with gratitude, their presence.

*Coffee and donut socializing hours following Sunday Masses have become a regular part of Catholic life.

*An increasing number of parishes send volunteer lay persons out each weekend after Masses to carry Communion to the housebound, thereby bringing them closer in spirit to the parish, and reminding healthy parishioners of their responsibility, to reach out toward all who are hurting.

*Most parishes today have some type of human development or Christian service committee, which works in diverse ways to help the poor or others in any kind of need. This may range from a local food pantry to collections for poorer parishes, from alcoholism counseling to bereavement assistance.

THE VERTICAL OR SACRED DIMENSION

While the theory and ideal, as well as efforts on the parish level like the ones just noted, promote the sense of belonging or community within the church, some Catholics today still fail to feel that they do belong to a welcoming, caring, community-oriented church. This is due to many factors, three of which I would like to note here: four centuries of a contrary tradition, the transcendent or sacred dimension of worship, and the self-centered tendency of our wounded human condition.

□ □ □

1. Four centuries of a contrary tradition.

The ritual book for Mass published in 1570 continued a clergy-dominated worship service pattern which had originated in the Middle Ages. Lay persons obviously were presumed to be present and provided for according to this format, but the priest performed almost every function. The role of people in the pews was to watch, listen, believe and pray. They were, generally speaking, mute observers.

Those years of silence created a comfortable habit for people. Sunday morning worship thus became a time for individualized silent prayer and awesome adoration, even though strengthened by the surrounding presence of many other believers.

When the Church, beginning in the early 1900's, officially encouraged congregational singing, active participation and communal-type activities at liturgical functions, lay persons found this foreign to their customs. Many, moreover, became uncomfortable or resisted leaving their more quiet, privatized practices during worship.

2. Transcendent or sacred dimension of worship.

While the liturgy or public worship has a horizontal or communal *we* direction, it also necessarily possesses a vertical, transcendent or *I* orientation.

I believe, pray and offer my adoration of God as an individual, even though joined with others in common prayer. Moreover, when I gather with others for worship, it is not merely for mutual fellowship or shared friendship, but also perhaps primarily, to offer to God gratitude and adoration, to manifest my dependence, to express my needs. In addition, this encounter with an awesome, transcendent, though loving Creator is wrapped in mystery. Like people who drew close to the Old Testament God or powerful Maker, we need to remove our sandals, bow down to the ground and remember our place.

Combining, as we should, both the vertical and horizontal elements or attitudes in the liturgy will always entail a certain tension with a tendency to emphasize one or the other. Before Vatican II, Catholic worship stressed the vertical or transcendent; after Vatican II, Catholic worship emphasized the horizontal or communal. Integrating the two requires a proper awareness and correct sense of balance.

3. Self-centered tendency of our wounded human condition.

Since the original sin portrayed by Adam and Eve, we all struggle with our weaknesses and an inclination toward self-centeredness. Catholics who arrive at Mass or other liturgies are no exception. Preoccupied with our own world and own concerns, we may have little desire to open up and extend ourselves to those around us.

This may manifest itself by wanting to remain in the back of church, not up front; to sit alone, not next to another; to pray in silence and not sing with others; to resist exchanging a gesture of peace with those around us; or to resent being forced to watch a stranger's baby being baptized during Sunday Mass.

There has been enormous growth in the community dimension of Catholic worship and parish life, but for the reasons we have just outlined, it is an on-going challenge. The sense of belonging which flows from that awareness will, as a consequence, seem at certain times and places either to flourish or to flounder.

PART OF A WIDER CHURCH

The church for most Catholics is identified with the parish to which they belong or at which they worship. However, while the parish is the basic unit of the Church with the pastor as the leader or shepherd of that community, both parish, pastor and parishioners are linked by an intricate system with all other Catholics in the world and to the Holy Father or Pope in Rome.

The parish normally covers a specified geographical territory, and all Catholics living within that region automatically belong to this particular church. The pastor is in charge of the parish; he is sometimes assisted by one or several other priests known as associate pastors or parochial vicars.

Some priests have the honorary title of *Monsignor*, (French for *My lord*) conferred by the Pope for distinctive service. The title does not necessarily indicate any special position, power or responsibility.

A **diocese** with the **bishop** as its chief shepherd is a collection of parishes and other Catholic institutions, usually covering several cities and counties in a state. A cluster of

dioceses is honorarily presided over by an archbishop whose primary responsibility is toward his own diocese (termed an archdiocese). While exerting natural influences over the bishops within his area, he does not possess true authority over them.

After the Second Vatican Council, most countries established coordinating bodies which link together all the dioceses of a country. In the United Sates this is called the National Conference of Catholic Bishops with a central office in Washington, D.C. The full body of bishops meet once or twice a year. They may not, however, make regulations which bind individual bishops except in specific matters expressly noted by the Pope.

The Holy Father or Pope unites all of these dioceses and bishops together in his position as bishop of Rome and successor of Peter. He is assisted in this monumental task by many offices in the Vatican. In addition, the College of Cardinals, a body of about a hundred bishops from around the world appointed by him or his predecessor, serve as consultors to the Pope and, after his death, select a successor to him.

The term *Catholic* in the phrase, *"I believe in the Holy Catholic Church,"* means *universal*, worldwide and all-embracing. When persons become members of the Roman Catholic Church through Baptism, they also begin to belong to a body of believers extending all over the earth. However, in most circumstances and on most occasions, they will experience that spiritual belonging in a parish and at Sunday worship. It is there and then that, surrounded by persons united to them by faith and grace who are meant to care for one another, they truly feel welcome.

CHAPTER 9

Yearning to be Free

THE CHALLENGE

Two teenagers were riding around the city on a motorcycle in the late afternoon.

The rider shouted over the noise of the engine that they should head for his home. When the driver asked why, the other reluctantly explained that his parents had told him he must be back at a specific hour. The driver shrugged, but changed directions and several miles later stopped at a corner near the younger man's house.

After exchanging farewells, the rider slowly trudged on home, his face a picture of negative feelings: disappointment that he could not continue on the bike with his friend and annoyance that his parents were curbing his freedom with strict regulations.

The motorcyclist roared away, seemingly carefree and unfettered. But his pensive expression revealed that he, too, was feeling irritated, or at least unsettled, by this sudden turn of events. However, the driver disclosed the real and perhaps surprising cause for his distress when he muttered to himself, *"I wish I had parents who cared that much."* 43

THE RESPONSE

We humans are a curious lot. Like the two young men, we on one level resent any restriction upon our freedom, but on a deeper plane want definite rules or regulations for our lives. We, at some moments, insist on *doing our own thing*, but at another time complain about a lack of direction from those in authority. We jealously guard our choices, but then wish someone would give us stronger guidance to keep us from making bad decisions and misusing our freedom.

The Church, as the first chapter noted, teaches that God gave us free wills. While our Creator watches over, protects, helps and influences us, we remain always free to say *yes* or *no*, to choose right or wrong. Although many factors such as family background, cultural surroundings or current circumstances may diminish the degree of our freedom and thus our responsibility for certain actions, we remain free to decide for good or for evil.

Understanding this mysterious reality of human freedom—that an all powerful, all knowing, all loving God allows us freely to use (or abuse) our world—helps to explain one aspect of the problem of evil in the world: the aspect of one human being's inhumanity to another.

In the face of world or local tragedies, people may ask, *"How could God do this to me, to us, to them?"* For example, the alcoholic dying of a diseased liver, the family torn apart by an episode of sexual abuse, the families of victims killed or maimed by terrorist actions may say, *"Why, Lord?"*

God could respond with these words, "I don't like or want those evils that people do to others. But I do not exercise my power to prevent them. For me to act otherwise would take away human freedom, for if humanity is free only to do good, then you are not truly free. However, my promise is that I will always keep working these bad

things around in your life and ultimately bring good out of them."

TRUE FREEDOM

Not all that glitters is gold, the old saying goes, and that applies to every human action. What seems immediately attractive and alluring can in time prove to be destructive and disastrous. Yet at the initial glance, wrong doing does appear to offer us something very desirable. In the words of a song, *"Sin is delicious."*

But after passion has run its course or the dust has settled around us, we usually discover that the bad choices, far from freeing us and buying true happiness, tend to enslave us and cause lasting sorrow.

We eat excessively and poorly; but eventually after a complete physical, we hear the doctor warn us about being overweight, about ominous blood test results, and about an emerging bad heart condition.

We drink too often and too much as an escape from challenges which face us; later we discover that becoming such an alcoholic *runner* solves no difficulties and creates additional stress.

In mid-life we foolishly pursue a strong attraction, thus violating our marital promises; finally we find that the new relationship has not made us truly happy and has further complicated our lives.

God's plan is a path which leads to true freedom and real happiness. That road may initially strike us as restrictive and pleasure killing; but in time, we recognize that the Creator's rules actually free us and increase our joys.

Nevertheless, we often experience difficulty in discerning this divine plan. The environment in which we live frequently holds up values that are in opposition to God's design for us. Our wounded, weakened human nature can strongly lean toward evil instead of the good; our

confused minds may mix up darkness and light.

As helps in understanding God's plan, the Creator has given us two guides: our conscience and the Church.

CONSCIENCE AS OUR GUIDE

Our conscience is not a tablet or a book which contains marks indicating good or bad behavior. Nor is it some other being inside us giving orders, issuing warnings or presenting awards.

Instead, conscience is a judgment of our minds about past, present or future behavior. We say within ourselves, *"This is a good choice and I did or should make it; that is a bad choice and I should not have made it or should not follow it in the future."*

Our conscience judgments may flow over into our feelings, but not necessarily. We may feel guilty about a poor choice or feel good about a positive one, but not automatically. Conscience is essentially a judgment of the intellect.

The following paragraph from the Vatican Council II document on the **Church in the Modern World** summarizes the Church's teaching today on the nature of our conscience:

Deep within our conscience we discover a law which we have not laid upon ourselves but which we must obey. Its voice, ever calling us to love and to do what is good and to avoid evil, tells us inwardly at the right moment: do this, shun that. For we have in our heart a law inscribed by God. Our conscience is our most secret core and our sanctuary. There we are alone with God whose voice echoes in our depths. By conscience, in a wonderful way, that law is made known which is fulfilled in the love of God and of one's neighbor. Through loyalty to conscience, Christians are joined to others in the search for truth and for the right solution to so many moral problems which arise both in the life of individuals and from social relationships. Hence the more a correct conscience prevails, the more do persons and groups turn aside from blind choice and try to be guided by the objective standards of moral conduct
(Article 16).

The Church helps us form correct consciences by clearly providing those objective standards of moral conduct.

GUIDANCE OF THE CHURCH

The Church, as we have seen, views itself as the Risen Christ living in the world today, carrying on his teaching, directing and saving mission. It, therefore, obviously looks to the words of Jesus first and foremost to establish those objective standards of moral conduct. The teaching of Jesus Christ is summarized in the two great commandments which have their echo or roots in the Old Testament or Hebrew Scriptures.

A lawyer, in an attempt to trip him up, asked him: "Teacher, which commandment of the law is the greatest?" Jesus said to him: You shall love the lord your God with your whole heart, with your whole soul, and with all your mind. This is the greatest and first commandment. The second is like it: "You shall love your neighbor as yourself." On these two commandments the whole law is based, and the prophets as well. (Matthew 22:36-40)

In your Bible, check the book of Deuteronomy 6:4-5 and the book of Leviticus 19:18 to locate the Jewish origin of those two commands.

During his public preaching, as recorded in the gospels and the New Testament letters, Jesus spelled out some of the implications arising from those two great commandments. According to Christ's words, to observe these imperatives means seeing Christ himself in any burdened person who is without clothes or food or who is confined in jail or sick at home; it means forgiving those who have hurt us; it means believing, praying and trusting; it means having pure hearts and doing good deeds.

But Christ also further specified the meaning of these two great commandments of the Old Testament. In response to a young man's question about obtaining everlasting life, the Master said, *"If you wish to enter into life, keep the commandments."* When the youth sought further clarification, Jesus responded by quoting Exodus 20:12-16 and Deuteronomy 5:16-20, sections which contain the ten commandments.

Thus, the Church likewise stresses the ten commandments with all their implications, as additional objective standards of moral conduct.

CONTEMPORARY APPLICATIONS

The two great commandments and the ten commandments, plus the scriptural teachings of Jesus, clearly offer substantial guidance for followers of Christ. Nevertheless, there have been and are now, and always will be, particular and complex moral issues for which our consciences require further direction and information. In response to that need, the Church over the centuries has built up, under the guidance of the Holy Spirit, a massive and detailed body of principles and aids to help form a correct conscience. For example:

*Jesus said that unless we eat his body and drink his blood, we cannot enter the heavenly kingdom. The Church to insure our compliance with these words of the Lord, requires that Catholics receive Communion at least once a year during the *Easter Season* from Ash Wednesday until Trinity Sunday. The Church encourages Catholics to receive the Eucharist every time they participate at Mass.

*The third of the ten commandments tells us to keep holy the Sabbath day. The church applies this rule through its regulation that Catholics have a serious responsibility to participate in Mass every Sunday.

*Christ preached about our need to deny ourselves, to be detached and to fast on occasion. Church law today maintains that as a minimum we must fast two days a year, abstain from meat on Fridays of Lent and have no food or drink one hour before Communion.

COMPLEX QUESTIONS

However, in addition to these laws governing Church matters, there is the much more complicated area of modern day moral challenges.

Is the practice of living together before marriage consistent with Jesus' teaching?

How do we harmonize Christ's absolute prohibition of divorce with the high rate of marital breakups and remarriage in our society?

Would the Master approve of genetic engineering?

Can we say that nuclear power, with all its risks as well as blessings, is part of the divine plan for us?

state universally binding moral principles found in the teaching of the Church; at other times the pastoral letter makes specific applications, observations and recommendations which allow for diversity of opinion on the part of those who assess the factual data of situations differently. However, we expect Catholics to give our moral judgments serious consideration when they are forming their own views on specific problems.

FREEDOM IN CHRIST

Catholics believe that an individual's conscience is the ultimate determinant of what is wrong or right for that individual. Moreover, God will judge us according to the fidelity with which we have followed our conscience. Nevertheless, this conscience needs to be formed by objective standards of moral conduct. The Church provides us with just that—moral norms based on Jesus' teachings, the inspired scriptures, centuries of tradition and the laws of nature.

These moral standards may seem at times to be inhibiting or restrictive. The fact is, that quite to the contrary, they release or liberate us. These norms both make us free, and lead us to the deep happiness which comes from following God's plan. Jesus underscored that point when he said: *"If you live according to my teachings, you are truly my disciples; then you will know the truth, and the truth will set you free."* (John 8:31-21)

Must a member of the armed forces refuse to fire a gun or drop a bomb because some innocent persons may be killed?

Are affirmative action laws Jesus' way of correcting past injustices?

The Church attempts to say something about all these matters. Nevertheless, while it can clearly state the commandments and almost as strongly teach certain general principles based upon the commandments, the further away the Church moves from the commandments and the more specific the issue at hand, the less authoritative the Church becomes. The Church on such points proposes its teachings more as tentative probings and studied insights designed to help Catholics resolve these delicate conscience questions. Here are two illustrations, first of a strong, then of a probing, proclamation of the Church.

EXAMPLE 1.

The commandments, Jesus' words and the New Testament scriptures generally speak about the appropriate use of sex. However, they do not clearly or explicitly deal with artificial contraception, direct sterilization, abortion, euthanasia, masturbation, premarital sex or homosexual acts. The official Church in various contemporary declarations seeks to give guidance on those particular points and judges these teachings as quite authoritative or binding.

EXAMPLE 2.

Jesus and the scriptures offer limited insights about many intricate questions connected with war and peace. The American bishops, wrestling over such related crucial concerns as the costly arms race and possible nuclear annihilation, published in 1983 a pastoral letter on war and peace, **The Challenge of Peace: God's Promise and Our Response.** However, in this case, the bishops explained in their introduction the kind of authority the document possessed:

As Catholic bishops we write this letter as an exercise of our teaching ministry. The Catholic tradition on war and peace is a long and complex one; it stretches from the Sermon on the Mount to the statements of Pope John Paul II. We wish to explore and explain the resources of the moral-religious teaching and to apply it to specific questions of our day. In doing this we realize and we want readers of this letter to recognize, that not all statements in this letter have the same moral authority. At times we

CHAPTER 10

Making Up and Starting Over

THE CHALLENGE

Some authorities on human communications describe the breakdown or even breakup of a relationship in four stages: distancing, gossiping, forgetting and hardening.

John and Donna, ages seventy and sixty-nine, would very likely agree with that analysis based on their own experience in forty-six years of married life. They recently had another blowup between themselves, and the cause for the crisis centered, as it usually does in marital spats, on something really vital or major: a garden rake.

DISTANCING

Neither spoke to the other for ten days. Moreover, she stopped cooking for him or doing his laundry, and he would not take her any place, a refusal which curtailed Donna's mobility since she cannot drive.

GOSSIPING

Both found willing friends or colleagues (he at work, she in the neighborhood) who would listen sympathetically to their angry accounts of their misunderstanding and probably would add some fuel to the fire.

FORGETTING

During this rupture, John and Donna forgot the positive qualities of the other and blocked out all the good times in the past. Yet, the husband did reluctantly admit to a peace-making daughter, *"I know your mother is a good woman and*

I couldn't make it without her." And the wife conceded that the girl's father wasn't all bad.

HARDENING

During this protracted cold war, their hearts hardened and their spirits stiffened, leaving no openness for mutual forgiveness and reconciliation. *"I am not getting down on my knees before your mother and admit I was wrong,"* John told his daugher. Donna spoke to her in much the same way.

This elderly couple have not separated or divorced. Eventually they made up and once again, for the umpteenth time in their long marriage, started over.

The real motivation behind this reconciliation was probably not so much Jesus' words about forgiveness, but more the simple fact that John missed his meals and Donna grew weary of staying in the house.

THE RESPONSE

We may well chuckle over this story of such a major dispute about such a minor concern, but those smiles might be prompted by the truth that we recognize ourselves in John and Donna's seemingly silly quarrel. However foolish their or our disputes, the pain of separation and distance during these moments is no laughing matter. Alienation, misunderstanding or rejection always hurts.

Moreover, the pattern of alienation and reconciliation, of hurting and healing, of breaking down or breaking up and then making up or starting over is an on-going experience for every human being, continuing until we die.

It should hardly surprise us, therefore, that Christ, and the Church he established, should both so frequently preach about the need for forgiveness and offer many powerful examples of people who forgive.

JESUS' WORDS AND EXAMPLES OF FORGIVENESS

Jesus spoke often about forgiveness. He quite bluntly told his listeners: **"If you forgive the faults of others, your heavenly Father will forgive you yours. If you do not forgive others, neither will your Father forgive you."** (Matthew 6:14-15)

The Master, nevertheless, repeatedly mentioned how anxious God is to forgive us:**"I tell you, there will likewise be more joy in heaven over one repentant sinner than over ninety-nine righteous people who have no need to repent."** (Luke 15:7)

Jesus also offered himself as a model of one who forgives.

During his three hour agony on the cross, Christ said, **"Father, forgive them; they do not know what they are doing."** (Luke 23:34)

THE CHURCH'S WORDS AND EXAMPLES OF FORGIVENESS

The Church naturally follows in the footsteps of its founder.

It preaches constantly about our need to forgive one another and to ask forgiveness from God and from each other. At the same time it unceasingly reminds us of God's ready willingness to forgive us.

*   At every Mass, the community recites or sings the Lord's Prayer and thus is reminded again and again, *"Forgive us our trespasses as we forgive those who trespass against us."* The exchange or gesture of peace follows soon thereafter. *"Let us extend to one another a sign of peace."* Worshipers may then smile, shake hands, embrace, kiss or wave as they say to one another, *"Peace be with you."* This is not intended merely to be a friendly gesture, but a rite of reconciliation preparing us for our approaching Communion with the Lord. Before being one with Christ in the consecrated bread and wine, we must first be one with our sisters and brothers. The persons around us to whom we offer a greeting of peace should represent or symbolize those with whom we have any differences.

*   At the beginning of most Masses, the presiding priest invites us to pause silently for a moment and consider our sinfulness, turning to the Lord in a spirit of repentance. Immediately thereafter, we together express in different formulas our contrition or sorrow for

past poor choices. For example, *"I confess to almighty God, and to you, my brothers and sisters, that I have sinned through my own fault . . ."* The ritual directs us to strike our breast at that point as a sign of our contrite hearts.

* Throughout the Mass in both the text of the prayers for each day and the scriptural passages which make up the readings, the message of God's eagerness to forgive comes across loud and clear. On Palm Sunday and Good Friday, the Church proclaims a scriptural account of Jesus' passion and death, the ultimate example of forgiveness and reconciliation. After Christmas we celebrate the feast of St. Stephen, the deacon martyr who, as he was being stoned to death, fell to his knees and cried out,*"Lord, do not hold this sin against them."* *(Acts of the Apostles 7:60)* Throughout the year we honor different saints of various centuries and countries, all of whom mirrored that spirit of forgiveness.

SIN: THE CAUSE OF ALIENATION

When we fail to follow our conscience and omit something which our conscience commands, or do something which our conscience forbids, we sin. That sin, or our state of sinfulness, ruptures multiple relationships in our lives. It weakens or severs our connection with God, with one another and with the world around us. It also upsets our inner harmony or peace.

Those serious conscience violations which totally break our relationship with the Lord are called, in traditional Catholic terminology, *mortal* sins. They cause us to lose now the life of divine grace within us, and unless they repent, they will exclude us from never-ending life with God in eternity.

Lesser conscience violations, which weaken but do not break our relationship with the Lord, are termed *venial* sins because they are more easily forgiven or healed. They do not fundamentally sever our friendship with God and would not exclude us from the eternal life to come.

The various norms for good moral conduct described in the last chapter give us guide posts and measuring rods for determining both what is objectively wrong and what is the degree of that wrongness. For example, Church teaching maintains that stealing a large amount of money would be a serious injury or wrong, while appropriating a small amount would be a lesser injury or wrong. Both actions are objectively evil, but the degree of wrongness varies.

Sin, however, is always subjective and depends upon the person's awareness and freedom. Thus, only God and the individual can judge whether a sin is mortal or venial, serious or lesser. More accurately, we could say God alone makes that ultimate judgment.

REPENTANCE AND RECONCILIATION

We need but to read the daily newspaper and to reflect on our own weaknesses to realize that we live in a sinful world. This could and does cause discouragement at times, but Jesus' words promise that God's mercy far outmatches our mistakes.

When Christ started preaching in Galilee, his first message was, *"Reform your lives and believe in the gospel!" (Mark 1:15)* Gospel is an old English word which means *good news* and the good news is that message of forgiveness. Nevertheless, God's mercy carries with it a price tag: our willingness to reform, repent or change our ways, to turn away from sin and back to God. Once we have done this, however, the gates of God's forgiveness instantly open up.

The Catholic church has always taught that as soon as we sincerely repent and seek the Lord's mercy, all our sins are forgiven. It consequently teaches and encourages every member to approach God directly through Jesus and ask for forgiveness. God forgives us in this way, very likely much easier and faster than we can comprehend. Yet, normally there remains within the human person burdened with guilt, a great need to express verbally her or his wrongdoing and to experience actual forgiveness through some word or gesture. For this reason, Jesus gave us a sacrament to meet that need.

CONFESSION, PENANCE OR RECONCILIATION

The Church's sacrament of Penance, also called Reconciliation or confession, provides an exceptional opportunity for this. It is called Penance from the root basis of that word which means a change of heart, conversion or repentance. It is called Reconciliation from the fact that this sacrament repairs multiple ruptured relationships with God and others. It is called confession because the sinner in some way confesses his or her wrongdoing(s).

Through this sacrament, repentant persons not only have occasion to disclose their sins but actually to experience the mercy of God who through the words and gesture of the priest forgives their sins. At the conclusion of the exchange between priest and penitent, the confessor extends his hands over the person, or toward the individual, and recites these words:

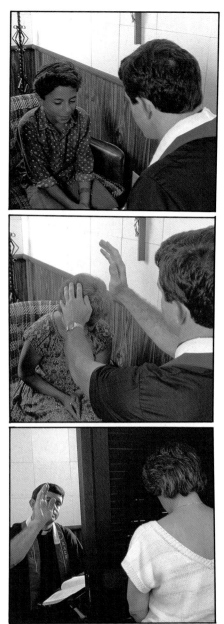

God, the Father of mercies,
through the death and resurrection of his Son
has reconciled the world to himself
and sent the Holy Spirit among us
for the forgiveness of sins;
through the ministry of the Church
may God grant you pardon and peace,
and I absolve you from your sins
in the name of the Father, and of the Son,
and of the Holy Spirit.

The priest understands that the secrecy of the confessional is most sacred and that he is forbidden ever to tell the sins of a particular person to anyone else. Priests, despite their other weaknesses or failures, have a remarkable history of observing and preserving the *seal of confession.*

Since the Second Vatican Council, most Catholic churches in the United States now include rooms or chapels of Reconciliation which provide penitents with the option of confessing anonymously behind some type of partition, or sitting face to face across from the priest.

In addition, several times a year, especially during Lent or Advent, parishes conduct communal Penance services. These attract a crowd of people and feature community song, prayer, scriptural passages, reflection and contrition followed by an opportunity for private reconciliation and absolution of sins.

Catholics are required to confess to a priest only their serious or mortal sins; they are, however, encouraged also to mention lesser or venial sins as a means of helping them to overcome their vices and to grow in virtues. Normally, a person burdened with serious sin would be expected to confess or receive the sacrament of Reconciliation before receiving Holy Communion.

The ritual for confession today includes a rich variety of biblical passages and scripturally based prayers to enrich the celebration of God's mercy and forgiveness. Nevertheless, the changed heart is the essential element here, not any precise words or formula.

At the end of a confession, the priest assigns a *penance* to the penitent. This may be a prayer or some good deed and is intended to make up, as it were, for the sin committed. It is to help heal the wounds caused by the misdeeds and to assist the penitent along the path of goodness.

Parishes list regular hours in church for celebrating the sacrament of Penance, usually on Saturdays. However, priests are available at any time and in any place for Reconciliation or confession.

PARDON AND PEACE

Guilt is a terribly oppressive burden. It permeates our whole being, interrupts our sleep, takes away our joy, clouds our vision, drains our energy and cripples our labors. A contemporary psychiatrist maintains that unacknowledged and unexpiated guilt is the ultimate source of all inner turmoil.

The Catholic Church teaches that God wants us to be forgiven of real guilt and healed of false guilt. The Lord has provided a special sacrament of Penance to declare this forgiveness and assist with this healing, and the only requirements are faith in Jesus' mercy and a willingness to repent.

Alienation is a separate but connected and equally burdensome condition of life. The Catholic Church teaches that God seeks reconciliation not alienation, that the Lord wishes us to make up and start over, that Christ calls us all to mutual forgiveness. In addition, the Catholic Church practices in the liturgy what it preaches. In official worship, it reminds us of our need to forgive, helps us to ask for forgiveness and proclaims the Lord's mercy to us.

The Catholic Church also offers many models of forgiveness and reconciliation, not the least of whom is Pope John Paul II. Months after being seriously wounded by gunshot, he traveled to a Roman prison and forgave his would be assassin, urging him to start over and move on with his life.

CHAPTER 11

Strength in Our Weaknesses

THE CHALLENGE

Immediately afterward, while dismissing the crowds, Jesus insisted that his disciples get into the boat and precede him to the other side. When he had sent them away, he went up on the mountain by himself to pray, remaining there alone as evening drew on. Meanwhile the boat, already several hundred yards out from shore, was being tossed about in the waves raised by strong winds. At about three in the morning, he came walking toward them on the lake. When the disciples saw him walking on the water, they were terrified. "It is a ghost!" they said, and in their fear they began to cry out. Jesus hastened to reassure them: "Get hold of yourselves! It is I. Do not be afraid!" Peter spoke up and said, "Lord if it is really you, tell me to come to you across the water." "Come!" he said. So Peter got out of the boat and began to walk on the water, moving toward Jesus. But when he perceived how strong the wind was, becoming frightened, he began to sink and cried out, "Lord, save me!" Jesus at once stretched out his hand and caught him. "How little faith you have!" he exclaimed. "Why did you falter?" Once they had climbed into the boat, the wind died down. Those who were in the boat showed him reverence, declaring, "Beyond doubt you are the Son of God!"

(Matthew 14:22-33)

THE RESPONSE

A priest was asked by his classmate to preach at a Mass celebrating the silver anniversary of their ordination to the priesthood. In his homily, he recalled this meeting between Jesus and the terrified apostles. The sermon concluded with these words:

"In the days ahead may you never hear the wind, may you never see the waves, but may you always keep your eyes fixed upon Jesus Christ!"

STRENGTH IN OUR WEAKNESSES

We have already mentioned in several contexts the weakness of our human condition and the constant struggle we face in our attempts to walk faithfully in the footsteps of Christ.

Jesus predicted that daily conflict and urged us to pray for the strength to emerge victorious. *"If you wish to be my follower,"* the Lord said, *"you must deny your very self and take up your cross each day." (Luke 9:23)* Christ also warned Peter and us, *"Be on guard and pray that you may not be put to the test. The spirit is willing but nature is weak." (Mark 14:38)*

However, God promises in the scriptures to give us all the help we need to overcome our weaknesses. In Paul's first letter to the Corinthians he says, *"The Lord will not let us be tested beyond our strength. Along with the test, God will give us a way out of it so that we may be able to endure it." (10:13)*

In his second letter to the same Christian community, Paul mentions that three times he had begged God for deliverance from some burden, some *thorn in the flesh.* But the Lord's response was, *"No. My grace is enough for you, for in weakness power reaches perfection."* St. Paul, hearing this, then

shifted his attitude: *"And so I willingly boast of my weaknesses instead, that the power of Christ may rest upon me . . .for when I am powerless, it is then I am strong." (12:7-10)*

THE SACRAMENTS

Jesus taught certain religious truths that we are to believe and pointed out a guided path through life that we are to follow. But Christ also instituted, or established, special means as events which supply that sufficient grace that God has promised, that power which makes us strong despite our weakness.

The Catholic Church calls these unique instruments of grace the **seven sacraments** and explains that they are outward signs instituted by Christ to give grace.

* As **outward signs,** those specified actions, words and objects point to something beyond. They are visible signs of an invisible reality or visible signs of invisible grace. We experience water, bread, wine, oil, hands, gestures and words; but looking beyond the external, we recognize God's presence communicated through these signs.

* When we say that the sacraments were **instituted by Christ,** we do not imply that Jesus established every detail of the ceremony for each sacrament. Instead, we hold that Jesus established the Church and empowered it to develop these seven unique signs as powerful occasions of God's presence. There are some direct references to certain of the sacraments in the scriptures (e.g. Baptism and the Eucharist), but not clear mention of them all.

* The purpose of these seven signs is to **give grace.** The word **grace** comes from a Latin word meaning gift or favor. The grace received through these sacraments is therefore a gift from God. This gift of grace communicates to us a sharing of God's life, together with special helps to fulfill our responsibilities as Christians. Three of the sacraments, Baptism, Confirmation and Holy Orders, confer, in addition, a permanent spiritual effect which makes the recipient, respectively, a member of the Church, a confirmed Christian, or an ordained priest (deacon or bishop). These three consequently, cannot be repeated.

As we briefly name and describe the seven sacraments, it will be evident how they match the major mo-

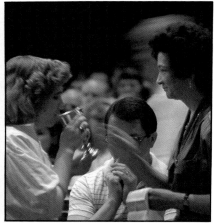

ments of our lives and also respond to the need for preserving the human race and the Church.

BAPTISM

A New Life and a New Family. In an earlier chapter we discussed how Baptism communicates Christ's life to the individual and also is the first stage of initiation into the Church as a community of believing Christians.

The baptized person usually has two godparents who agree to assist the parents in the task of raising the child as a Catholic Christian. Ordinarily, the godparent must be over sixteen and an exemplary, fully initiated Catholic. However, a non-Catholic who is a baptized and believing Christian (e.g., Lutheran, Methodist, Presbyterian, etc.) may act as a Christian witness as long as there is a Catholic godparent or sponsor as well.

When adults already truly baptized in other Christian communities wish to enter the Catholic Church, they are not rebaptized, but instead simply recite a profession of faith in their new spiritual home.

CONFIRMATION

Gift of the Spirit. At Pentecost the frightened followers of Christ were transformed by the power of the Holy Spirit into fearless preachers of the Lord's victory over death. Confirmation is seen as that Pentecost event renewed today, as well as a complement to Baptism leading on to the Eucharist.

Generally speaking, young people receive the sacrament in their midteens after one or two years in a multi-dimensional preparation program which includes study, prayer and projects of service to others.

Adults entering the Church are usually confirmed when they receive Baptism or make their profession of faith. The local priest confirms in those cases, but otherwise a bishop ordinarily ministers the sacrament of Confirmation.

The essential ritual consists of a prayer invoking the Holy Spirit accompanied by the bishop's or priest's outstretched hands. The candidate is anointed on the forehead with the oil of chrism as the celebrant says, *"Be sealed with the gift of the Holy Spirit."*

The candidate also has a sponsor, who ideally is the same person as the godparent for Baptism, thus showing the connection between those two sacraments.

THE EUCHARIST

Worship, Food and Presence. There is an essential difference between the Eucharist and the other sacraments: The other six communicate the grace of Christ; the Eucharist contains Christ himself.

Traditionally the Church views the mystery of the Eucharist from three approaches: First, it is the perfect worship of the Father through the Spirit in Christ, the unbloody, representation of Jesus' sacrifice for us on the cross. Second, it is Jesus' true body and blood which we receive as spiritual food under the sign of bread and wine. Third, it is the Lord's real presence maintained in the tabernacle for later distribution to the sick and for personal prayer or adoration.

Since the Eucharist is so central to the life of the Church, we have used different portions of the Mass—the Eucharistic Celebration—throughout this book to illustrate Catholic teaching and practice.

The fundamental elements of the Eucharist, of course, are bread and wine plus the narrative words from Jesus' Last Supper with his disciples, now pronounced by the priest, *"This is my body . . . This is my blood . . ."*

Receiving the body of the Lord in the symbol of bread or wine is a sign of full membership in the Church and implies personal ac-

ceptance of all the Church's teachings. This act is called Communion. Ordinarily, therefore, only Roman Catholics in good standing may receive Communion. Conversely, Catholics may not ordinarily receive Communion at services in other churches of different traditions.

PENANCE

Forgiveness and Growth. We examined at some length this sacrament of healing and grace in the last chapter.

ANOINTING

Healing, Courage and Hope. The ritual book for this sacrament, *Pastoral Care of the Sick,* contains two parts—one for the sick and the other for the dying:

The first section provides prayers to be recited for and with the sick, a rite for bringing Communion to those who are ill and the format of the actual sacrament for the anointing of the sick.

A priest ministers the actual sacrament of Anointing to those who are seriously ill by laying hands upon their heads in silence. He then anoints their foreheads, hands or other hurting parts of the body with a specially consecrated oil of the sick and recites this form:

Through this holy anointing may the Lord in his love and mercy help you with the grace of the Holy Spirit. May the Lord who frees you from sin save you and raise you up.

These words plus surrounding prayers and biblical passages indicate the purpose of the sacrament: to communicate the grace of the Holy Spirit to those who are sick, to help the ill persons bear their sufferings, to restore the sick to health and to forgive a recipient's sins.

The second section includes a rite for Communion for those who are critically ill or near death and a series of beautiful prayers for those who are dying.

The Church urges that the sick confined indoors have an opportunity to receive Holy Communion frequently, even daily, and especially on Sundays. Furthermore, to make this possible it encourages lay persons to assist the clergy in bringing Communion to the sick and praying with them.

MATRIMONY

Building the Little Church. The five sacraments noted above correspond to certain life cycle needs of individuals: birth, growth, maturity, sin, sickness and death. These last two, Matrimony and Holy Orders, in a sense have a more social dimension. The former insures the continuation of the human race and the later, the continuation of the ministry of Jesus.

Matrimony differs from the other sacrament in that the man and woman minister the sacrament to each other by their public exchange of vows; the priest or deacon stands as a witness of the Church to these promises of exclusive and permanent fidelity until death. Throughout their married life, the couple can expect Christ's presence and assistance at every moment. In addition, as they live out their vows, the husband and wife bring the Lord into their midst in a unique way.

The Church, following the words of Jesus, disapproves of remarriage after divorce. Nevertheless, it also recognizes that frequently in our modern world a man and a woman, with the best of intentions, enter a marriage without awareness of their lack of certain essential elements that make a marriage a sacrament. Each diocese has an office, termed the marriage tribunal, which studies those situations and, where warranted, grants a declaration of nullity which frees both to marry again in the church. That annulment process is never initiated, however, until the parted couple has obtained a legal separation or divorce.

To eliminate potential marital disasters and facilitate better marriages, dioceses and parishes offer a variety of marriage preparation programs. In many areas the engaged couple is required to attend one of these programs before the sacrament will be celebrated.

HOLY ORDERS

Continuing the Larger Chruch. Through this sacrament a bishop ordains or sets aside certain men to function as bishops, priests or deacons. This ordination thus provides an essential element needed for the perpetuation of the Church. There is a separate ritual for each of these ministries with its own appropriate prayers, readings and blessings; but all three ceremonies include the laying on of hands and a precise prayer formula.

Immediately before the Second Vatican Council there were only *transitional* deacons—men receiving this order as a step toward the priesthood; after Vatican II the Church restored in addition a tradition of *permanent* deacons—usually married men—who promise to serve in a unique and committed way for the rest of their lives.

Deacons, permanent and transitional, today assist the presiding priest or bishop at the altar. They baptize, witness marriages, conduct funerals, preach, teach, and normally engage in some activity, or several activities, to help the hurting.

The priest, in addition to his role as teacher and leader, is designated as a presider over worship. In that capacity he can celebrate most of the sacraments. While the deacon also ministers some, only the priest offers Mass, grants absolution in the sacrament of Penance, and anoints the sick.

The bishop possesses all the graces and designation of deacon and priest, but in addition he may ordain others to Holy Orders and is the ordinary minister of Confirmation.

Two vital and controverted questions about Holy Orders receive much attention today: *mandatory celibacy* (or the required non-married status for priests in most of the Roman Catholic Church) and the *ordination of women.*   57

The law mandating celibacy for the clergy is clearly only a Church regulation and therefore, theoretically, it could be modified or dropped at any time. However, this rule has a long tradition. Local legislation requiring the unmarried status for all priests and deacons dates back as far as the late fourth century. This became a universal regulation in the Church around 1200.

Supporters of the celibacy requirement for the clergy judge that the unmarried state frees the priest for more available service to others and also manifests, through this voluntary sacrifice of a natural and desirable good, faith in a supernatural good—the life to come.

There are advocates, significant in number and background, who currently press for a change which could make celibacy optional. However, Pope John Paul II has, to this point, rejected that proposal even though in exceptional circumstances he has permitted some married men to be ordained for the priesthood.

The *ordination of women* as priests or bishops is a more complicated issue. The Church seeks to be faithful to the mind and teaching of Jesus. The fact is that throughout the history of the Church no woman has ever been ordained as a bishop or as a priest, at least as we understand those positions today. There have been, however, ordained deaconesses (wives of deacons) and women deacons.

Does this absence of any example of ordained women priests or bishops reflect the intention of Christ? Or does it simply mirror a sexist bias of society throughout these two millenia of Christianity? Until the official Church becomes convinced, through study and reflection, that this unbroken tradition reflects something other than Jesus' thinking, it will not change its policy and extend ordination to women.

Nevertheless, several Church documents in the United States have urged an increasing involvement of women in all other areas of Church life, including key leadership positions. Those recommendations have already been put into practice in many circumstances on both the parish and diocesan level.

A SACRAMENTAL PEOPLE

All of the sacramental rituals include a gesture known as the laying on of hands. It is very obvious in Confirmation, Penance, Holy Orders and Anointing of the sick, but can easily be detected in the other three sacraments as well. That ancient gesture extends back into the Jewish tradition and to other religions before Christ. It symbolizes that the person upon whom hands are laid, is set aside for a special task and is given the power to fulfill his or her responsibility.

Through the laying on of hands in the sacraments we are set aside, consecrated and directed to imitate the example of Christ. This symbolic gesture also conveys the grace of God, which strengthens us in our weakness and enables us to fulfill our duties as Catholic Christians.

CHAPTER 12

Coping with Life's Hard Knocks

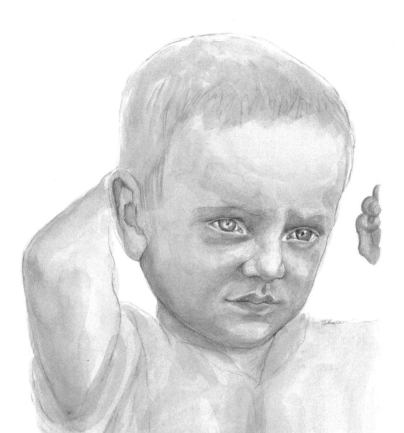

THE CHALLENGE

Aaron Kushner was a bright and happy child who at the age of two could identify different kinds of dinosaurs and explain with patience to inquiring adults that dinosaurs were extinct.

However, his father (a Jewish rabbi) and his mother had been concerned about the tiny tot's health from earliest days, particularly when he stopped gaining weight at eight months and when he began losing hair after one year.

Distinguished doctors examined the boy and put a complicated scientific name to his condition; they assured the anxious parents that Aaron would grow to be very short but, otherwise, quite normal.

Around the time of his third birthday, the family moved to a Boston suburb where Rabbi Kushner assumed responsibility for a local congregation. There the parents learned of a pediatrician researching problems connected with the growth of children and asked for his analysis of Aaron's situation.

Several months later, the specialist informed them that their child had progeria, or "rapid aging." The doctor more specifically predicted "that Aaron would never grow much beyond three feet in height, would have no hair on his head or body, would look like a little old man while he was still a child, and would die of old age in his early teens."

Aaron, in fact, died two days after his fourteenth birthday leaving behind sorrowful, angry parents with many unanswered questions about a good God who could afflict such pain upon people, or fail to cure such a cruel disease.[1]

THE RESPONSE

The tragedy of Aaron Kushner's life and death is a unique, dramatic story, and like the demise of any teenager it not only inflicts pain, but also unsettles all those touched by the event.

Nevertheless, the rabbi and his wife would certainly be the first to admit that many, many others have suffered, and do now endure, equally devastating burdens. One need only possess an interest in people and a willing ear to learn of the diverse and crushing hard knocks in life with which individuals are trying to cope.

These can range from the health problems of a first born child to the deteriorating mental state of an elderly parent, from the drug related disaster of a teenage offspring to the unpredictability of an alcoholic spouse, from the destruction caused by a flood to the depression brought on by unemployment.

The Catholic Church, both in its teachings and practices, provides effective help for such afflicted persons. It offers to them powerful prayer, supportive people and hopeful truths.

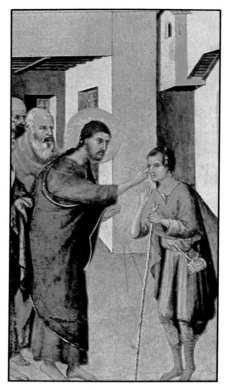

POWERFUL PRAYER

The Church takes seriously Jesus' promise that if we ask for anything in his name it will be done for us. Bolstered by this assurance, it prays formally and publicly for people with burdens and urges members to speak with God in personal and private prayer about their needs.

For example, in the sacramentary or book of prayers for Mass there are over 2,000 prayers which cover almost every conceivable situation. One generic prayer **"For Any Need"** reads this way:

All-powerful Father
God of mercy,
look kindly on us in our suffering.
Ease our burden and make
our faith strong
that we may always
have confidence
and trust in your fatherly care.

As another example, we might cite the General Intercessions or Prayers of the Faithful each Sunday at the

Eucharist. This series of petitions mentions the needs of people in the parish and throughout the world. Then, after each request the total community responds with a common plea such as *"Lord hear our prayer."*

Jesus predicted at the end of Mark's gospel that those who believe in him and use his name will have the power to lay their hands upon the sick and witness their recovery. Aware of this prediction, an increasing number of Catholics in our times are carrying out that practice as a parish, in groups, within the family and on an individual basis. Here are examples of that prayer for healing:

* Once a month after Sunday Mass in certain churches, those who wish to come forward to the altar, are prayed over by the clergy and designated lay persons.

*Charismatic groups feature as a standard part of the regular prayer meetings a laying on of hands with petitions for the healing of those burdened in any way.

*Some dedicated families bless one another with a sign of the cross each day, and pray specifically for those not feeling well.

*It is common today for individuals visiting the sick, to lay hands upon them or trace a cross on their foreheads and explicitly pray for their recovery.

SUPPORTIVE PEOPLE

Even if the sick do not actually regain their health or the difficulties afflicting a person do not disappear (and remarkable recoveries or resolutions frequently have occurred), this prayer for help always heals. An inner calm or mental uplift inevitably results. Part of that interior serenity, or renewed spirit, certainly develops from the mere presence of a caring, supportive person who touches and prays for the burdened individual.

Throughout history, there have been groups of Catholics particularly dedicated to works of mercy and service. These *religious* people, both clergy and lay, men and women, chose to remain celibate and to live a community life, professed vows of poverty, chastity and obedience, and served in a particular field like health care, education or missionary preaching. They came to be known as sisters (nuns) or brothers (friars), or—if they were clergymen—religious order priests. For almost half of the Church's history, most of the charitable and educational work of the Church was done either by the local clergy or by these *religious* women and men. In general, lay women and men did perform some part-time acts of charity, but traditionally,

only clergy and religious carried out these responsibilities as the major purpose of their lives.

However, the Second Vatican Council triggered an explosion of lay persons undertaking full and part-time labors within the Church. The bishops at Vatican II explicitly mentioned that lay persons—through their Christian initiation by Baptism, Confirmation and Eucharist—have both the right and responsibility to build a better church and a better world. The particular fields in which they do the work of the church now tend to be termed *ministries*, those carrying out the tasks are called *ministers*, and the training process for them is known as *ministry formation*.

Naturally many of those efforts and ministries aim directly to relieve burdens, assist the needy and heal the hurting. Here are a few illustrations:

*The parish schools that are often attached to larger Catholic parishes were once staffed almost entirely by religious women. Today, many

parish schools have no *religious* staff at all. This education *ministry* is increasingly an apostolate of the laity. The salary of these dedicated teachers is often one-half to two thirds of the equivalent public school salary.

*A New Jersey parish identifies people who have been through certain burdens and are willing to share their experiences or insights with others, then lists their names and phone numbers in the church directory. There are several dozen categories in this un-salaried, *One-to-One Ministry,* from alcoholism, to adoption, to suicide and to terminal illness.

*More and more churches have groups of people, paid staff or volunteers, who visit the sick, dying and grieving on a scheduled basis with the hope that no Catholic will ever suffer, die or grieve alone.

*Youth ministry staff in many, if not most parishes, are lay people who are especially interested in youth and who have the rapport necessary to relate to young people.

HOPEFUL TRUTHS

Even with powerful prayer and supportive people, however, burdened persons still ask *"Why?"* What is the reason behind this tragedy? How could God do this to me or to us? The Kushners wrestled in agony with that issue, pondering why bad things happen to good people or how a supposedly good God is connected with such obviously bad events.

The Church does not offer a simple, pat answer to those perplexing questions. But it does provide insights that shed some light and hope for those in darkness and near despair. What follows below is one person's statement of faith regarding the mysteries and challenges that mark our lives:

*We bring on much suffering by our own sinfulness and mistaken decisions.

*Others cause us suffering by their actions which may or may not be sinful.

*God wishes to eliminate through us, human pain and suffering.

*Much suffering, once attributed to inexplicable forces beyond us, is discovered later to have a human origin.

*Those tragedy-producing events, like earthquakes, tornadoes, and hurricanes, apparently beyond human control, are mysteries which we cannot fathom but they still fit, somehow, into God's overall plan of love for us.

*God's goodness, love, and concern for us are absolutely certain, unconditional, and all-embracing.

*The Lord is actively present in our midst, working on and with and through us for our good and the good of others.

*God brings good out of everything in our lives, especially our sins, mistakes, and troubles.

*Suffering, borne bravely and with acceptance, possesses a mysterious power to help others.

*All of life and, in particular, life's troubles are best understood and most successfully endured in the context of the life to come.[2]

The Ultimate Healing

We saw earlier that God wishes us to be happy here and to share our happiness with others. We share our spiritual richness, as well as our material wealth and security, by our mission efforts to extend the faith and by our social involvement to extend the justice that God planned for all humanity. At the same time, the Church never wants us to forget that we are on a journey, that we are but pilgrims in a foreign country, and that all questions will be answered, all burdens lifted, all pain removed and all sorrow turned to joy. The ultimate healing and complete explanation will take place in heaven.

Death is essentially the departure of our own immaterial soul or spirit from our material body. The physical remains immediately begin to deteriorate, but the spiritual soul is indestructible and goes before God face to face for an instant review of one's life and to determine one's destiny for eternity. The body at the end of this earthly world will finally, in some mysterious way, be raised up and rejoined to its partner soul forever, either in glory or in damnation.

The Church dramatizes a belief in the sacredness and destiny of the body in its funeral practices and ritual. The Church prefers burial in consecrated ground, following the example of Christ, rather than cremation. However, cremation is permitted, providing this decision by the survivors does not reflect a disbelief in resurrection. Burial, rather than scattering, of the ashes is expected.

During the actual ceremony the priest or deacon sprinkles the body with holy water as a reminder of Baptism, and the casket is covered with a decorated white cloth recalling the baptismal garment. Then the casket is incensed as a sign of respect for the body, the temple of the soul.

The Church teaches that our final destination, depending upon the way in which we have lived our lives, will be either heaven or hell. If we die having rejected God totally by our sinful lives and unrepentent of our evil, contrary choices, the Church maintains there is no alternative but for the Lord to confirm our decision to negate all that is good, all that is life-giving. This means separation from God forever in a situation we call hell. The essential pain in hell is an awareness of our great loss and eternal absence from God's loving presence.

While the Church has proclaimed that certain particular persons are in heaven, it has never declared any specific individual to be in hell. While Jesus revealed there is a state of hell for any who reject him, Christ has also told us that he wills for us all to be with him forever. Reconciling those two revelations is another mystery we cannot grasp here, and thus the questions of whether any person is in hell, or how many are there, are unanswerable.

For those who die repentant, but have not made up for their sins or purified their hearts, the Church believes in a state of purification after death called purgatory (from a word meaning "purify"). Even though that name developed only in the 13th century, Christians from the very beginning manifested their faith in this state of purification by praying for those who had died.

We cannot help those in hell and those in heaven do not need our prayers. But the Church has continued that tradition, started by the first Catholics of *praying for the souls of the faithful departed,* and being conscious that they can pray for us. The month of November is specially dedicated to the *holy souls* and November 2 is the feast of All Souls Day.

When a person dies, Catholics normally bring or send a *Mass card* as a sign of sympathy. These cards are obtained from a local parish where the person makes a nominal offering for the Church and requests that a Mass be offered for the person who has died. These requests are usually printed in the weekly bulletin and the name of the deceased often mentioned at the General Intercessions.

The ultimate goal for all of us is heaven. During the funeral liturgy the Church underscores our hope for this in many ways. The readings speak of resurrection and life; the prayers point toward our eternal happiness with God; the lighted Easter candle reminds us of how the Risen Jesus conquered forever darkness and death; the music has a victorious tone to it; Holy Communion brings to mind Christ's promise that those who eat his body and drink his blood will live forever and that he will raise them up on the last day.

In heaven we see God face to face, experience inexpressible joys, and find our hearts totally fulfilled.

PEACE AND JOY

What it means to be a Catholic, both here on earth and hereafter in heaven, is rather nicely summarized in a morning prayer from the Church's official prayer book or Liturgy of the Hours. (Friday, Week IV).

Lord,
fill our hearts with your love
as morning fills the sky.
By living your laws
may we have your peace in this life
and endless joy in the life to come.